The Poetry of
JOHN CROWE RANSOM

Truman Moore

The Poetry of
John Crowe Ransom

Miller Williams

 RUTGERS UNIVERSITY PRESS
New Brunswick, New Jersey

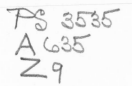

Copyright © 1972 by Miller Williams
Library of Congress Catalogue Number: 78-184566
ISBN: 0-8135-0712-X
Manufactured in the United States of America by
Quinn & Boden Company, Inc., Rahway, New Jersey

Permission to reprint has been kindly granted by the following publishers:
Louisiana State University Press: *Southern Writing in the
Sixties: Fiction,* edited by John W. Corrington and
Miller Williams (1966)
Meridian Books: *On Modern Poets,* by Yvor Winters (1959)
The Swallow Press: *The Function of Criticism,* by Yvor
Winters © 1957, Chicago

Contents

Acknowledgments

I am grateful to Mr. Ransom and to Alfred A. Knopf, Inc., for permission to reprint from the copyrighted edition of *Selected Poems* by John Crowe Ransom (1969). All mention of particular poems by Ransom refer to those poems as they appear in the 1969 edition of the *Selected Poems,* except where the 1963 edition is specifically indicated.

The Poetry of
JOHN CROWE RANSOM

The Man, the Poet

Few have had as much to do with the molding of this country's literature as John Crowe Ransom. Among those who were his students, in or out of the classroom, or who worked with him, under his influence and tutelage, are Donald Davidson, Allen Tate, Robert Penn Warren, Cleanth Brooks, Andrew Lytle, Robert Lowell, Thomas Merton and Randall Jarrell. He stands now not only as one of the best lyric poets of our time, but as the first spokesman for the New Criticism and philosopher of the old religion.[1]

Ransom was born the thirtieth of April 1888 in the small town of Pulaski, Tennessee. His father, John James Ransom, was a Methodist preacher, a self-educated man who had gained some reputation as a linguist and a scholar. He had returned from missionary work in Brazil to marry Miss Ella Crowe.

As Methodist preachers' families—especially those serving smaller churches—are frequently moved from one town to another, interrupting the school year and upsetting what formal schooling might be available, Ransom was taught at home by his father until he was eleven. Then he became a student in the Bowen School in Nashville, where he studied Latin and Greek and discovered the excitement of intellectual discussion.

3

When he was fifteen, he passed the formidable examinations required for entrance to Vanderbilt University. He soon distinguished himself in the classics and philosophy and was named a Rhodes Scholar in Literary Humanities.

It was at Oxford that he encountered modern poetry for the first time, and though it was radically removed in its rhythms and images, its immediacy and common metaphors, from the classical poetry he had grown up with, he developed a great enthusiasm for it.

Home again in 1914, he was offered a position in the English Department at Vanderbilt and accepted the challenge of working outside the area of his formal studies. He earned a reputation as a superb teacher and became the magnetic center of a group of students who had been meeting from time to time for intellectual and literary talk. Donald Davidson invited Ransom to attend the meetings of the group, which at the time consisted also of Sidney Hirsch, Nat Hirsch (Sidney's younger half-brother), William Yandell Elliott, Alec Stevenson and Stanley Johnson. All were students, teachers, or townsmen.[2]

With the outbreak of World War I, Ransom and Davidson both volunteered for service. Ransom was eventually sent to France for four months as a first lieutenant of infantry. Davidson, a second lieutenant, reached France in time for some heavy fighting in the last days of the war.

After the war Ransom studied at Grenoble, where he finished his first volume of poetry, entitled *Poems about God*. He sent the manuscript of the book to Christopher Morley, who had published some of the poems in a column he edited in the Philadelphia paper, *The Evening Public Ledger*. Morley passed the manuscript on to Robert Frost, who recommended it to his publishers, Henry Holt and Company.

The book appeared to fair notices in April 1919, before Ransom's return to Vanderbilt in September of that year, when the old group formed again almost intact. The most important change was the addition in 1921 of Allen Tate, a senior who had earned a reputation as a brilliant and well-read student.

By this time, things were beginning to stir in that South which H. L. Mencken had called, not without some justification, "the

4

sahara of the Bozarts." In the year in which Tate joined the fort-
nightly group, whose members were then writing as well as talking about poetry, the year after Mencken had written that a poet
was "almost as rare in the South as an oboe-player, a dry-point
etcher or a metaphysician," three new literary journals appeared.
From New Orleans, Richmond and Norfolk came *The Double
Dealer, The Reviewer* and *The Lyric,* respectively. In 1922 the
Nashville group published the first issue of their own magazine,
which they called *The Fugitive.*

The title was taken from a poem by Hirsh, and though it
seemed a good name for the magazine, somehow appropriate, the
members of the group never made clear what its implications
were. Or at least they never agreed publicly on any single implication. It was suggested that the group was fleeing everything
from "the high-caste Brahmins of the Old South" [3] to sentimentalism to "the extremes of conventionalism, old and new." [4]
Publication of the magazine continued into 1925, by which time
the circle included its youngest member, a red-haired student
named Robert Penn Warren. He had been invited to join in the
spring of 1922, his sophomore year at Vanderbilt.

The Fugitive ceased publication with the fourth number of
the fourth volume, dated December 1925. The group continued
to meet, with a shifting membership, for three more years.
Cleanth Brooks became a member shortly before the group dis-
integrated in 1928 as the participants left Nashville for new jobs
or to further schooling in various parts of the country.

Out of the *Fugitive* phenomenon came a reassertion of the
value of lyric poetry in a time of experimentation in the directions of imagism, vers libre and fragmentation, and in a time
when any lyricism was bound by association, in the minds of
many, to gross sentimentalism and conventional, imitative and
easy ways. The phenomenon gave rise ultimately to a critical
attitude set forth in Ransom's book *The New Criticism* (New
Directions, New York, 1941), in Brooks's *Modern Poetry and the
Tradition* (University of North Carolina Press, 1939) and *The
Well Wrought Urn* (Reynal and Hitchcock, New York, 1947).
The approach to poetry exemplified by these works, an approach
which was essentially formalistic, was quickly labelled "The New

5

Criticism" and brought about not only a revamping of the teaching of poetry in the schools and colleges of the United States, but strongly influenced the work of the majority of American poets for over forty years.

Although Ransom had published three more books of poetry, the philosophical work *God without Thunder* (the original publisher was Harcourt, Brace and Co. in 1930) and the philosophical-critical work *The World's Body* in 1938, in 1939 he was pressed by professional and economic factors to move to Gambier, Ohio, where he taught at Kenyon College and founded *The Kenyon Review*. When he retired in 1959, the *Review* (since discontinued) was the leading literary journal in the nation.

Ransom's total output of poetry is not large; his considerable reputation as a poet rests on the work he did over a period of less than eight years, but out of those years have come a disproportionate number of the poems contained in the standard anthologies of our day.

After *Poems about God* in 1919 came *Chills and Fever* in 1924, *Grace after Meat,* published in London the same year, and *Two Gentlemen in Bonds* in 1927. His *Selected Poems,* which first appeared in 1945, was revised and enlarged in 1963 and again in 1969.

Chills and Fever included far more than its share of what later constituted the *Selected Poems* and may contain more excellent poems than any other single book by an American poet: "Spectral Lovers," "Bells for John Whiteside's Daughter," "Winter Remembered," "Vaunting Oak," "Miriam Tazewell," "First Travels of Max," "Emily Hardcastle, Spinster," "Necrological," "Armageddon," "Judith of Bethulia" and "Captain Carpenter" were all introduced in this one volume. The Pulitzer Prize in Poetry for 1924 went to Robert Frost for *New Hampshire, A Poem with Notes and Grace Notes.* Ransom was finally honored with the National Book Award in 1964 for the second edition of *Selected Poems.*

Ransom is a poet as the Greek scholar in him would understand the word. He is a maker. His poems are contrived, structured, not to appear as moments torn almost intact from the actual lives of actual people. There is no attempt at realism;

rarely does his dialogue afford an illusion of conversation. Ransom doesn't mind that we can see the underpinnings to the art that the welding shows. This is not theater-in-the-round. The proscenium arch is elaborately there, and we imagine that his characters are obliged now and then to step to the footlights and in the manner of Restoration actors declaim a few lines to the audience.

Ransom's poems are mostly about domestic situations; this is perhaps because in the familial he finds the condensation of those questions, essentially theological, which ultimately are the only questions worth asking.

What Ransom treats in his poetry are those concerns which hold the attention of every sensible person: sex, death and religion. Sex here, of course, encompasses all of that which belongs to romantic love, marriage, home-building and childbirth as well as the frustration and satisfaction of the libido. It is the primary life-force and is responsible for the very existence of the man and the woman whose fealty it commands. Death puts an end to that force, and religion attempts to make sense out of both death and the sexuality which tries desperately to overcome death and to make sense out of existence itself, which is anchored to sex at one end and to death at the other.

Sex and death are treated more or less directly. Religion may be a presence, visible or invisible, but just as Ransom would tell us that theology as a human concern is involved in everything we do, so it is in every poem he has written.

It should be noted here that Ransom's concern with death—and he has devoted a larger part of his work to this subject than most poets—is not only with death as a dark reality which has to be examined; he is concerned not so much with mortality itself as he is concerned with the proper attitude toward mortality. The noblest characters in his poems are stoic, standing with Ransom in that tradition of the Southern Calvinists which we call Christian stoicism. Ransom dislikes any flagrant emotional display, especially of grief, as such a display reveals at least a temporary dissociation of sensibility, a breakdown in that bond of mind and spirit whose integrity Ransom cherishes.

But what strikes a reader on first coming to Ransom's poetry is neither the theme nor the metaphysics. It is the language, an idiom that seems to echo at the same time the classics, the King James Bible, medieval ballads and Southern preachers. Randall Jarrell supposes—and surely he is right—"that the quality of Ransom's rhetoric . . . was suggested by his profession, by Oxford, by the lingering rhetoric of the South, by the tradition of rhetoric in the ministry, and by his own quite classical education and interests." [5]

This rhetoric serves the poem in a number of ways, but probably the most important is the laying of an aesthetic and emotional distance between the poem and the reader. Any direct expression of emotion—especially the gentler feelings—is always dangerous in a poem. In the period when Ransom was writing it was especially so. This was the time of the imagists, of the publication of *The Waste Land*. The experimenters in taste and technique were moving to the hard line, the tough and violent. It was necessary to find some sort of scrim to cover the naked feelings of love, loneliness, compassion, sorrow. But this is only half of it; Ransom was not *forced* into hiding. If there had been no imagists and no Eliot, he still would have muted his feelings, would have kept us from getting too close to the subjects of his poems. Because that would be indulgence, would play dangerously with pain and pleasure. And Ransom is stoic.

Of Ransom's poems, none is more typically his, embodies more of those elements by which we recognize his handiwork, than "Necrological," a small story of a good friar and the world as it is.

NECROLOGICAL

The friar had said his paternosters duly
And scourged his limbs, and afterwards would have slept;
But with much riddling his head became unruly,
He arose, from the quiet monastery he crept.

Dawn lightened the place where the battle had been won.
The people were dead—it is easy he thought to die—
These dead remained, but the living all were gone,
Gone with the wailing trumps of victory.

8

The dead men wore no raiment against the air,
Bartholomew's men had spoiled them where they fell;
In defeat the heroes' bodies were whitely bare,
The field was white like meads of asphodel.

Not all were white; some gory and fabulous
Whom the sword had pierced and then the gray wolf eaten;
But the brother reasoned that heroes' flesh was thus;
Flesh fails, and the postured bones lie weather-beaten.

The lords of chivalry lay prone and shattered,
The gentle and the bodyguard of yeomen;
Bartholomew's stroke went home—but little it mattered,
Bartholomew went to be stricken of other foemen.

Beneath the blue ogive of the firmament
Was a dead warrior, clutching whose mighty knees
Was a leman, who with her flame had warmed his tent,
For him enduring all men's pleasantries.

Close by the sable stream that purged the plain
Lay the white stallion and his rider thrown,
The great beast had spilled there his little brain,
And the little groin of the knight was spilled by a stone.

The youth possessed him then of a crooked blade
Deep in the belly of a lugubrious wight;
He fingered it well, and it was cunningly made;
But strange apparatus was it for a Carmelite.

He sat upon a hill and bowed his head
As under a riddle, and in a deep surmise
So still that he likened himself unto those dead
Whom the kites of Heaven solicited with sweet cries.

"All poetry," Stewart reminds us, "stands at no less than one
remove from the experience it treats. . . . Much of Ransom's
poetry stands at two removes from the experience, for instead of

looking directly at life he has, in many instances, looked into other works, into the Bible, Shakespeare, sermons, bestiaries, seventeenth-century lyrics, nineteenth-century novels and children's stories." [6] The view and the rhetoric, drawn from such a various array of times and places, work in the poems to build a world like nothing else we have known. Or are likely to know. Because, although Ransom has been a great influence as a man of letters, he has had no perceptible stylistic influence through his poems. He has written in a style too much his own for anyone to imitate without copying slavishly. So to understand Ransom, to read him well, we have to go to Ransom. When we do, we see a poet who has known as few have, even in his time, the meaning of tension in verse. We see the poet as the balancer of force; the poet as equilibrist.

Ransom is, and has been found from his earliest publication, opposed to the science-oriented mentality of this century and an enemy of rational positivism. He has been called reactionary, romantic, and decadent. He is a poet of such skill, compassion and elegance, however, as to confound such critics.

It is not possible to read Ransom's poems well without the whole person in mind, Southerner, Calvinist, scholar, poet and man, as the parts come together repeatedly in all of the poems. The observations made in the following sections are meant to be understood in terms of this attitude toward the man and his work; they are to be taken as particular functions of the generalities outlined here, as it is hoped that the subsequent sections will show how the attitudes of Ransom inform and illuminate the poems.

Donne wrote of the shock of science, the way in which it can put "all in doubt," and man has always been most disturbed by that scientific "revelation" which seems to threaten his self-esteem. But Ransom has not been concerned with this. He has come to mistrust "science" because of the fact that the world of science must of its nature be a world of abstraction, and because he rejects abstraction as a way to any good end.

He is not concerned much with whether science has moved man further from the center of things. In any case, while at first the discoveries and concepts of Copernicus, Kepler, Galileo, New-

10

ton, Pavlov, Darwin and Freud were humbling to man, the continued development of scientific knowledge has brought man the awareness that he is capable of destroying all life on earth, has taught him to transplant hearts and kidneys and fly to the moon, so that science is seen more and more as a magnification of man. Ransom's view of the world and his poetry therefore come from the conviction that neither science nor abstract philosophy will avail to make sense of the world, and, while some sort of rational humanism might, this is an attitude for which this world has no use. The world is obsessed by what it cannot use and will not use what it can. To this awareness Ransom brings a Calvinism which denies that man's destiny, or for that matter his right, is to dominate the world he finds himself in. Calvinism is not a world-affirming attitude, but Ransom is more than a Calvinist; he is a poet, and if John Calvin keeps him from trying to master or manipulate the world, he does not keep him from knowing it and loving it. This is all man has left. And to the poet, knowledge and love depend finally upon man's sensibilities, his awareness of the points of contact between his senses and the concrete, phenomenological world.

He takes not a despairing but an ironic view of his inability to master, to overcome the world which is his and yet is not his, and in this ironic pose finds a comfortable detachment. This ironic detachment, in turn, enables him to keep both worlds—the desirable and impossible world of the scientist and the abstract philosopher and the inescapable and painful world of John Calvin and the poet—balanced one against the other.

In this balance of two worlds, this polarity, is the tension which gives shape and life to nearly all of Ransom's poems. In the joy of contact, the aesthetician's belief in the *things* of this world, comes the poetry's deeply satisfying sense of experiential reality.

Balance is the word which will probably surface most frequently in any discussion of Ransom's poetry. As Bradbury [7] puts it, "His humanistic training imposed on a traditional Methodist substratum had developed a habitually dualistic mode of thought. In his most characteristic utterances he opposes human reason to a nonrational natural order, which he accepts empirically. His recognition of Nature's indifference and mystery, however, is

11

tempered with a sensuous appreciation of her careless bounties and beauties. As a true humanist, he insists upon cultivation of both mind and body, senses and reason; he sets himself equally against puritan asceticism and irrational indulgence."

Scorning any hope of dominating the world by reason or by faith or by science, he comes instead to comprehend the world in a mythology which by the nature of its origin must render man's reason no reason and his contempt of what is just a foolish irrelevancy. The ancient Hebrew God was indifferent at best to man's reasons, as we are clearly told in the Book of Job. It is to the myth surrounding this God that Ransom returns.

He could not go a shorter distance. Christology replaced the God of thunder with another figure whose first concern was man's salvation, thus whose reason was man's reason and who was just as man would be just. Christ became history's most anthropomorphic god.

This is not to say that Ransom "believes in" the Hebrew God, as one believes in a round earth. He understands very well that truth and fact are not always the same thing, and he has cautioned us against confusing the two. His posited God he has called a "supernatural fiction," and he warns us that God does not, by our recognition of him, become therefore a "natural object."

Santayana knew this God, and Bradbury reminds us [8] that Coleridge, in his own light, did also. His "willing suspension of disbelief" constituted what he called "poetic faith," and that is precisely the faith of Santayana and of Ransom.

What Ransom rests with is that his thundering God need do no more for man than furnish the world with particularity, the stuff of experience, which experience can then be understood in terms of the myth surrounding that same God. But if this attitude, while satisfying to Ransom, seems perhaps a metaphysical or psychological error to others, it seems nothing less than moral error to still others. Probably Yvor Winters spoke best for these:

We may be interested in communism, cancer, the European war or Ransom's theories of poetry without liking any of them. According to Ransom's theories, the scientist does not

12

like, in this sense, the objective universe, but that he is desperately interested in the objective there cannot be the slightest doubt. If we like the poem, we like it because of the truth with which it judges its subject, and the judgment is a moral judgment. . . . Ransom's devout cultivation of sensibility leads him at times to curiously insensitive remarks. In comparing the subject of a poem by Stevens with that of a poem by Tate, he writes:

> the deaths of little boys are more
> exciting than sea-surfaces. . . .

a remark which seems worthy of a perfumed and elderly cannibal. And in a poem of his own, entitled "Bells for John Whiteside's Daughter," a poem which deals with the death of a little girl, the dead child herself is treated whimsically, as if she were merely a charming bit of bric-a-brac, and the life of the poem resides in a memory of the little girl driving geese. The memory, as a matter of fact, is very fine, but if the little corpse is merely an occasion for it, the little corpse were better omitted, for once in the poem it demands more serious treatment: the dead child becomes a playful joke, and the geese walk off with the poem.[9]

As I have remarked elsewhere,[10] it is perfectly obvious that Ransom is using "exciting" here in the way Amy Lowell used it in remarking that the role of poetry was to excite the consciousness. It is disturbing that Winters should imply that he did not realize this, but more disturbing is Winters' statement that "the dead child herself is treated whimsically, as if she were merely a charming bit of bric-a-brac, and the life of the poem resides in a memory of the little girl driving geese. . . . the dead child becomes a playful joke, and the geese walk off with the poem." I am at a loss for a reply to any reader who fails to see that the power and the pathos of the scene, the awful reality of the child's death, all live in the geese, the silly, white geese, and that this is consistent with the classic eye Ransom casts on death. The poetry, as Wilfred Owen would tell us, is in the pity. And the pity is in the image

13

of the sensate geese who will not recall the insensate girl. Understanding the poem is, indeed, a matter of sensibility.

Winters and his followers prefer abstraction. He says:

> For the past two hundred and fifty years it has been common to assume that abstract language is a dead language, that poetry must depict particular actions, or if it be "lyric" that it must be revery over remembered sensory impressions, according to the formula of the associations. But these assumptions are false. They are our heritage of confusion from Hobbes and Locke, by way of Addison, Hartley, and Alison —and more recently by way of Ezra Pound. A race that has lost the capacity to handle abstractions with discretion and dignity may do well to confine itself to sensory impression, but our ancestors were more fortunate, and we ought to labor to regain what we have lost. The language of metaphysics from Plato onward is a concentration of the theoretical understanding of human experience; and that language as it was refined by the great theologians is even more obviously so. The writings of Aquinas have latent in them the most profound and intense experience of our age. It is the command of scholastic thought, the realization in terms of experience and feeling of the meaning of scholastic language, that gives Shakespeare his peculiar power among the English masters of the short poem.[11]

On the other hand, not only Ransom and his confederates but John Ciardi, among others, has focussed on the problems of abstraction as opposed to the sensory line. Ciardi shares Ransom's suspicion of abstraction in poetry and states his case in this way in speaking of the inseparable twin of abstraction in writing, which is abstraction in reading: the practice of paraphrase:

> This immediately leads away from the form into something called meaning with a capital "M," or "significance" or "larger content" or "eternal verities"—all dangerous concepts when applied to the poem. . . . What determines the poem

14

is not the size of the subject, but the size of the mind that is engaged in the subject.

A fool could look at the universe and see nothing . . . but the most mind, the most intelligence, could look at an amoeba and project the universe from it.[12]

Thus Ciardi takes us back to the particulars with which Ransom builds his world and by which he knows it.

Perhaps it should be noted again that the myth-makers whom Ransom most admires—the Hebrews and the people generally to the east of the Hebrews—have not created gods who serve man's ends. Their gods remain indifferent to the ways and will of man. Ransom tells us, in fact, that the purpose of prayer to such a god is not to sway God to man's purpose, but to reconcile man to his "impending defeat." This is the view of pessimistic existentialism, which is the inevitable end of the loss of faith in science and abstract philosophy in a world which is obsessed by them. But we need not look to existentialism as such for this attitude; it is just as clearly Calvinistic, as Calvin is understood in the religious South. It is in terms of this Calvinism that Ransom is most Southern. It alone would possibly have turned him from scientism had he developed no philosophy beyond it. Science looks to the ultimate perfectibility of man; this is romanticism at its brightest. Southern Calvinism denies the possibility of the perfectibility of man and even denies the morality of his attempts at perfection, insisting that the most man without grace can hope for is to lose nobly, in whatever sense a person out of the grace of God can be noble. This is romanticism at its darkest. Bright romanticism and dark romanticism can no more exist in the same mind than the sun can seek out the night.

In the United States almost everyone, Catholic, Jew and agnostic as well as practicing Protestant, is Calvinistic in the very real sense that we have all been touched by the ethic and psychology of those pioneers who came to cultivate not only the soil but the spirit of the nation. In the South and especially in a Southern parsonage, people know that John Calvin has breathed the air they breathe, and his presence is a heaviness upon

15

it. When Ransom was a child, this was even more true than it is now.

What the Southern Protestant child takes in with that air is first of all a resignation to the inability of man to save himself either by works or faith. So he becomes stoic.

Then without knowing it, he acquires the conviction that he must one day face the Throne of God to answer for all his thoughts and actions; that no one else can, in any case, by any intercession, answer for him and that there is no answer. So he comes to a sense of responsibility for his own sins, and he becomes more stoic.

Then comes also the conviction that because man is removed from God, he has no right to pleasure; that to seek worldly pleasures outside the Garden is not only blasphemy, since it counteracts the sense of the expulsion, but is madness, since it compounds the sin for which man was expelled; that man should by all means seek instead to make himself acceptable to God should God in grace or whimsy choose again to examine man's composite soul. The Calvinist turns instead to Good Works, not so much to win the Lord's favor thereby, but to keep his mind and his hands from the pursuit of pleasure. Every good work, in this sense, is done for the glory of God, so that the Calvinist tends (as does, to some degree still, the Protestant in general) to become a compulsive worker, almost fearing idleness, and contemptuous of the lazy. A need to be "producing" is upon him all his waking hours, the need to act rather than to be acted upon, as the Old Testament Protestants remember the admonition that they be "doers of the word and not hearers only."

All this suggests to the Calvinist an unworthiness in the eyes of God and an abiding guilt. It is a guilt not only for Original Sin, for separation from God in the beginning, but for those personal sins that accumulate through the years like wrinkles in the flesh. So the Calvinist tends to be self-recriminating and to hunger for the redemption he believes he cannot deserve and has no way of earning.

It is virtually inevitable, then, that the Calvinist should be deaf to those who claim to offer man dominion over the world into which God has placed him, or freedom from toil or escape from

16

the final accounting. It is equally certain that such a person will be stoic in his attitude toward that world and then develop that sense of irony that makes such a condition bearable.

John William Corrington joined me recently in describing the religious nature of the South, especially the South Ransom knew, in these terms:

> To this day, the South is a religious land. There is no corner of the old Confederacy in which the unpainted clapboard church, the raw sermon steeped in hell-fire and brimstone, the unrelenting consciousness of God's sovereignty and man's insignificance, of original sin and current degeneracy, is not remembered. The King James Bible yet looms over the South as the Colossus of Rhodes towered over that ancient port. Its rhythms, its languages, its thoughts and its concepts of God's will and man's nature still hold in thrall the imagination. . . .
> But this religion is not simply ordinary American protestantism with a drawl. It is, by and large, that religion contemptuous of man's efforts and his achievements alike, a religion that denies man's ability to be co-partner in any enterprise with the divine—such as salvation. . . .
> The myth of unlimited progress, of man's perfectibility, never has had much currency in the South. Man's will weakened, his intellect darkened by original sin, is not the foundation for Utopia. . . . Neither damnation nor salvation depend . . . in any significant way upon a man's own acts. . . . Judgment is in God's hands. A man does what he must, worships and hopes. There is not much else to do.[18]

One aspect of Ransom's poetry which is occasionally associated with his Southern roots is the elegance of his language. Nowadays we rarely hear the word elegance used in the discussion of poetry, and almost always when it is used it is associated with decadence—whether in the France of Louis XIV or the Confederacy of Tara and Twelve Oaks. Possibly, however, this is an association not entirely founded in fact. Ransom is certainly a poet of the most natural elegance of language, and he came from

17

a South which he has known only in a state of decay, but the American poet most akin to Ransom in many ways, and certainly the poet turning the most elegant line after Ransom, is Richard Wilbur, born in New York City and raised on a country estate in New Jersey.

Perhaps before turning from the discussion of the South as it may bear upon Ransom's work—especially that South which Ransom saw decaying—we ought to look at what Ransom himself has said.

He asked, in 1935, whether "works of art [are] like . . . apples, reaching their best when the society behind them is under sentence of death." [14] In a letter to Allen Tate in 1927 he wrote that "our cause is, we [the fugitives] all have sensed this at about the same moment, the Old South. . . . I like my own people, or rather I respect them intensely. . . . Our fight is for survival." [15]

The "cause" was what Louise Cowan [16] refers to as their as yet vague plans "to stem the tide of the engulfment" of the South by creeping industrialism. The concern culminated in the publication of the book of essays entitled *I'll Take My Stand* (1930), a manifesto to which Ransom, Davidson, Tate and Warren, among others, contributed essays.

However, Ransom also remarked in a letter to Tate in 1930 that "I don't write consciously as a Southerner or as a non-Southerner," [17] and in another letter to him shortly thereafter added "About Rationalism and Noblesse Oblige: you do me the honor to let me be a mouthpiece for a very noble historic culture. But this is both accidental and perhaps the questionable feature of your interpretation of Ransom's work." [18] I suspect that such disclaimers indicate not that Ransom was moving away from his roots, the sense of the South and the ghost of Calvin but that he was already beginning to carry all of this with him in some supra-logical part of his being, as any man carries those most basic and pervasive elements of the society into which he was born and in which he grew to manhood.

The Poet as Equilibrist

In the discussion of tensions and ambiguity which has taken place during the past several years, the apparent influence of the seventeenth-century metaphysical poets on Ransom's poetry has been mentioned countless times. To emphasize this influence, I think, is to misread the poetry; it is not metaphysical except in certain of its effects. It draws considerably on the force created by the yoking together of what appear to be incompatibles, but the fairly extended forces in Ransom's work are not a result of those techniques generally thought of as metaphysical. The tension of his poetry lies not very much in the mutual repulsion of two elements of a metaphor, such as Dr. Johnson found to his displeasure in the poems of John Donne, or in the bristling of a poem against a "nonpoetic" language. Ransom is more skilled than most in these techniques, but his poems are charged with another and a stronger force. In almost every one of them, the stage is set between opposing thematic positions, and we find that we are unable to make a choice between them. The poet will not, and so the characters never can either. It is beneath this tension—the polarity of statement—that the minor stresses play through the poems.

One of his best-known pieces, "The Equilibrists," gives in its title, its structure and its texture a touchstone to the sources of this force, this peculiar power which we can call—as an inclusive term—the equilibrium-stress. In this, as in most of his poems, it is Ransom who finally is the supreme equilibrist. He gives us passion in perilous balance with honor—the polarity of statement, the major force. In the texture of the poem itself, the additional sense of balanced forces in the juxtaposing of warm Teutonic and sterner Latinate words, and in the use of slant rhyme, which come to our ears like the notes of close harmony repelling and attracting each other, in the alternate use of modern and archaic terms, the pageantry and the pedantry of the language, the homeliness and nobility of tone.

In "Here Lies a Lady," Ransom treats of the whole idea of unresolved polarity, the division (in the dissociation of personality) of those parts which ought to form a whole and apparently would have us believe that some sort of conciliation between the extremes is necessary, or anyway desirable. It is, in other words, a poem of moderation and compromise. So, in another way, is "The Equilibrists" a poem of moderation, if we can take the balance between two forces and the dominance of neither as a centering of the tension, a tug-of-war in which the rope never slacks and never moves one way or another. This surely, in Ransom's view, is a nobler compromise than the running back and forth between two extremes as in "Here Lies a Lady."

We are dealing primarily, in each of these poems, with polarity of statement, but "The Equilibrists" shows how thoroughly the equilibrium-stresses of the texture support the polarity of structure:

> Full of her long white arms and milky skin
> He had a thousand times remembered sin.
> Alone in the press of people traveled he,
> Minding her jacinth, and myrrh, and ivory.
>
> Mouth he remembered: the quaint orifice
> From which came heat that flamed upon the kiss,
> Till cold words came down spiral from the head,
> Grey doves from the officious tower illsped.

Body: it was a white field ready for love,
On her body's field, with the gaunt tower above,
The lilies grew, beseeching him to take,
If he would pluck and wear them, bruise and break.

Eyes talking: Never mind the cruel words,
Embrace my flowers, but not embrace the swords.
But what they said, the doves came straightway flying
And unsaid: Honor, Honor, they came crying.

Importunate her doves. Too pure, too wise,
Clambering on his shoulder, saying, Arise,
Leave me now, and never let us meet,
Eternal distance now command thy feet.

Predicament indeed, which thus discovers
Honor among thieves, Honor between lovers.
O such a little word is Honor, they feel!
But the grey word is between them cold as steel.

At length I saw these lovers fully were come
Into their torture of equilibrium;
Dreadfully had forsworn each other, and yet
They were bound each to each, and they did not forget.

And rigid as two painful stars, and twirled
About the clustered night their prison world,
They burned with fierce love always to come near,
But Honor beat them back and kept them clear.

Ah, the strict lovers, they are ruined now!
I cried in anger. But with puddled brow
Devising for those gibbeted and brave
Came I descanting: Man, what would you have?

For spin your period out, and draw your breath,
A kinder sæculum begins with Death.
Would you ascend to Heaven and bodiless dwell?
Or take your bodies honorless to Hell?

In Heaven you have heard no marriage is,
No white flesh tinder to your lecheries,
Your male and female tissue sweetly shaped
Sublimed away, and furious blood escaped.

Great lovers lie in Hell, the stubborn ones
Infatuate of the flesh upon the bones;
Stuprate, they rend each other when they kiss,
The pieces kiss again, no end to this.

But still I watched them spinning, orbited nice.
Their flames were not more radiant than their ice.
I dug in the quiet earth and wrought the tomb
And made these lines to memorize their doom:—

EPITAPH

Equilibrists lie here; stranger, tread light;
Close, but untouching in each other's sight;
Mouldered the lips and ashy the tall skull.
Let them lie perilous and beautiful.

There is a startling repulsion-attraction between the Anglo-Saxon "mouth" and the Latin "orifice," two words in one way identical and in another opposite and set against one another at opposite ends of the line. In the same stanza there is the juxtaposition of "cold" and "heat." Such juxtapositions happen repeatedly in Ransom's work and hint at what much of Ransom's poetry is about. It shows up again in the next to last stanza of the poem, where it is important that one be as radiant as the other.

With the use of "tower," Ransom begins to build a medieval scene, a tapestry which he works into several of his poems and which the poems, in fact, seem sometimes to become. The distance created in this way, especially when Ransom is dealing with such a subject as passion, gives us a sense of equilibrium between the past and the present, history and experience, so that here the lovers seem at once to be intensely alive yet living only in an ancient and illuminated manuscript, very much with us but long dead, barely recalled by the speaker. Randall Jarrell has said that "Ransom's poems are produced by the classical, or at worst semiclassical, treatment of romantic subjects." [19] Certainly that tension is here and is a strong one.

"Said-unsaid" is another use of equilibrium-stress. Making verbs negative in this way is one of Ransom's favorite stylistic devices. It adds a dimension to an idea which the ordinary form of expression lacks, as for instance in the difference between "I have not been loved" and "I have been unloved." The second carries the sense not of nothing done to me, but of something done which is contrary to love.

The polarity of statement is explicit in stanzas seven and eight, the halfway point—the fulcrum point—of the poem. All the force of the poem is focussed here, and in the next stanza, where the polarity is stated even more fully.

This is one of several poems ("Dead Boy," "Spectral Lovers," "Here Lies a Lady," "Of Margaret") in which Ransom keeps things in the third person, classically removed, for most of the poem's length, or enters as observer and reporter, then in the end puts himself into the poem, actually taking part. The distance is not destroyed by this, but the poem is given a pathos that would have been impossible had the poet been directly involved from the beginning. The poem then would have been not so much pathetic as maudlin.

Ransom often treats subjects which begin very close to sentimentalism and lean sometimes far over the edge before pulling back. This is especially evident in "Janet Waking," the story of a broken-hearted little girl whose chicken has died.

He is continually faced with the problem of keeping the presentation of the subject dry, while at the same time moving the reader as deeply as possible. It is a part of Ransom's genius that he so often does both. But involved as he is in "The Equilibrists," it is not easy to tell which side the poet is on, what choice he would have the lovers make. The absence of moral choice maintains the equilibrium, and we see that the loss of equilibrium would be the loss of tension and therefore death for the poem before the death of the equilibrists. Resolution of the balance in favor of either choice must be impossible.

Most frequently, Ransom builds his polarity by running romanticism, innocence or illusion, into a sudden, hard confrontation with reality, a conflict between what we want the world to be and what the world is. This is the structure of "Janet Waking," "Necrological," "First Travels of Max," "Vaunting Oak," "Blue Girls," "Captain Carpenter," and "Miriam Tazewell." There is something almost of Camus' absurdity in the collision of Miriam Tazewell's innocence and the world's fury, and it gives rise to the kind of ironic predicament that holds Ransom's mind in thrall.

When Miriam Tazewell heard the tempest bursting
And his wrathy whips across the sky drawn crackling
She stuffed her ears for fright like a young thing
And with heart full of the flowers took to weeping.

But the earth shook dry his old back in good season,
He had weathered storms that drenched him deep as this one,
And the sun, Miriam, ascended to his dominion,
The storm was withered against his empyrean.

After the storm she went forth with skirts kilted
To see in the hot sun her lawn deflowered,
Her tulip, iris, peony strung and pelted,
Pots of geranium spilled and the stalks naked.

The spring transpired in that year with no flowers
But the regular stars went busily on their courses,
Suppers and cards were calendared, and some bridals,
And the birds demurely sang in the bitten poplars.

To Miriam Tazewell the whole world was villain,
The principle of the beast was low and masculine,
And not to unstop her own storm and be maudlin,
For weeks she went untidy, she went sullen.

The storm, we are told, was not a catastrophe for the world; it was part of the order of things. Miriam, more is her pain, does not belong to the world. She is a neurotic woman with whom Ransom brings us—even so or therefore—to empathize. There are more than a few such people in Ransom's poems, people who have lost touch with whatever it is that might keep them resilient and sensitive, but not too resilient and not too sensitive, which is maybe what sanity is. The thing is that Ransom loves them, and in spite of ourselves so do we.

The implied sexuality of the assault is metaphorical and ironic. To Miriam, the most treasured of all things is her illusion, her belief in the world as it ought to be. She is virginal of mind and spirit and chaste in wisdom. The rape-metaphor was weaker in the 1963 version of the poem, in which the world was simply villain; in the 1969 version the world is also "masculine."

Ransom, too, goes in his lines untidy and sometimes sullen, breaks his tone of voice and speaks in a gray understatement, for the same reason as Miriam.

But if he has spent most of his words on the examination of illusion against reality, he is better known for his treatment of passion against honor, flesh against spirit. This is the polarity of "The Equilibrists," the poem that comes first to mind in this connection, and of "Spectral Lovers," "Good Ships," "Emily Hardcastle" and "Hilda." But even this is not of final importance. That balance which is for Ransom the most important of all comes with the terrible separation of sense and sensibility. These are the poles which charge the poems "Morning,"

> . . . before the true householder Learning
> Came back to tenant in the haunted head,
> He lay upon his back and let his stare
> Penetrate dazedly into the blue air . . .

and "Here Lies a Lady" (the lines quoted here are not all consecutive in the poem):

> First she was hot, and her brightest eyes would blaze . . .
> But that would pass, and the fire of her cheeks decline
> Till she lay dishonored and wan . . .
> And would not open her eyes, to kisses, to wine . . .

It's what's happening in "Painted Head":

> . . . the instinct of heads to be
> Absolute and to try decapitation
> And to play truant from the body bush . . .

and "Of Margaret":

> The generations born of her loving mood
> Were modes of yellow greenery, not of blood . . .

Other polarities are treated, less frequently but no less effectively, in "Bells for John Whiteside's Daughter" (the quick and the dead), "The Tall Girl" (sin and virtue), "Old Man Playing With Children" (youth and age), and "The Vanity of the Bright Boys" (that disparity between our image of ourselves and the world's image). These are important, and they are forceful poems. But none of them is as central to the mind of Ransom as those whose polarity is the very *idea* of polarity: the separation of sense and sensibility.

These categories are helpful when we want both a close look and a perspective, but it would not be less accurate to call most of Ransom's work a Poetry of Loss. This would include almost every poem he has written and cuts across the distinctions of subject matter and style. Because in the confrontations of illusion and reality, life and death, youth and age, hope and despair, the real world wins, death takes the young, despair settles in. Only in "Captain Carpenter" is the world's victory in any sense pyrrhic; here as always that is enough for the world.

Which is to say the polarity is not stable. One pole or the other gains dominance, so that at the end of the poems, even if the poet did not make a moral choice for us between the forces he has set up, there is a sense of resolution, of exhaustion, loss of charge. For there is loss of innocence, as in "Janet Waking," "Necrological," and "First Travels of Max." There is loss of hope of consummation, one of the most dominant ideas in Ransom's poetry. Jane Sneed says in "Eclogue," "We must not fructify," which is also the idea working in "Spectral Lovers," "Good

26

Ships" and "Emily Hardcastle." Loss of hope informs "Dead Boy" and "Vaunting Oak." The inevitable loss of the beautiful, the fragile and transient is told in "Lady Lost," "Of Margaret" and "Piazza Piece." Ransom also treats the loss of the past in "Old Mansion," loss of integrity in "Here Lies a Lady," and loss of love and comfort in "Two in August" and "Winter Remembered."

As for the loss of life itself, Ransom is among the best of the elegists in "Emily Hardcastle," "Hilda," "The Equilibrists" and "Dead Boy." And, of course, in Bells for John Whiteside's Daughter":

> There was such speed in her little body,
> And such lightness in her footfall,
> It is no wonder her brown study
> Astonishes us all.
>
> Her wars were bruited in our high window.
> We looked among orchard trees and beyond
> Where she took arms against her shadow,
> Or harried unto the pond
>
> The lazy geese, like a snow cloud
> Dripping their snow on the green grass,
> Tricking and stopping, sleepy and proud,
> Who cried in goose, Alas,
>
> For the tireless heart within the little
> Lady with rod that made them rise
> From their noon apple-dreams and scuttle
> Goose-fashion under the skies!
>
> But now go the bells, and we are ready,
> In one house we are sternly stopped
> To say we are vexed at her brown study,
> Lying so primly propped.

The almost nonconnotative "bruited," the humor of the geese scuttling "goose-fashion," lend the distance, the perspective the poem has to have, especially after such an opening line. We realize slowly that the poem is not a simple elegy, that the grief is not so great as the consternation and wonder. The "brown study" "astonishes" us; we are vexed, but we are vexed more at the turning of quickness into stillness than at the loss of the little girl herself, and we are taken most with the contrast between the stillness of the girl and the scuttling of the geese. Our understanding is incomplete, we are taken aback, and because of this—only Ransom's word will do—we are vexed.

There are a few other poems which have about them little or none of this, but whatever else he may have turned his lines to, Ransom, more than any other poet, has given form and substance to the sense of loss. And this is what the world—the modern world, at least—is about. Hemingway said it in most of his stories: The world will get you sooner or later; you aren't going to win.

So what a man can hope for is not to win, but to make what victory there is out of defeat. What a man can hope for is to lose on his own terms. It was what Hemingway kept saying. Ransom says it, too, in all his voices.

The forces, then, that give Ransom's poems their life come from the equilibrium-stress, which is primarily the polarity of statement supported and intensified by the minor stresses of the language. The pathos, the passion of the poetry is found in the losing: it lives in the inevitable passing away. This too, being as it is oxymoronic, irreconcilable, is a polarity creating tension, and so creating life, since for the poems, of course, as well as for the reader, that is what life is.

What Grey Man Is This?
Irony

A sense of irony is the abiding realization that every human statement contains its own contradiction and that every human act contains the seeds of its own defeat. From this comes the realization that there are no pure truths and that there are no pure men or pure women or pure causes or pure motives. There is neither the simply holy nor the simply unholy. John Calvin and Camus alike understood that man's very lot is one of awful irony, as he finds his rational self facing a nonrational universe, his hungering and homesick soul facing an incomprehensible and indifferent God. This is the terrible wisdom which moves perceptibly through Ransom's poems.

He gives irony its most dramatic expression in the polarity of statement. In "Armageddon" it is Christ who is bloodthirsty, while Satan tells us that he is weary of war and prefers the fellowship of good talk; the "Old Man Playing with Children" finds that he and the child are "equally boy and boy"; "The Equilibrists" are beautiful in their eternally unconsummated and undenied love; the Friar in "Necrological" becomes as one with the slain soldiers.

The several forms of irony are working all at once in Ransom's poems. What we have called simple irony, the tension between things as they seem to be or ought to be and things as they are, or between what is expected and what comes to be, is built into the structure of the last poem mentioned, as it is present also when we sense that "Judith of Bethulia" has a strange and permanent interest in the severed head of the enemy chieftain and might not have gone reluctant to the orgy.

It is present in "Vaunting Oak," when the tree—the "symbol of love"—responds to a knocking with a hollow and funerallike tone and in another way when we realize that the poem "Dead Boy" is not about the boy dead, the "first-fruits," but the tree's "sapless limbs, the shorn and shaken."

It is present, spelling out still something of Camus' absurdity, in the confrontation of Ransom's people and the real world they can neither ignore nor live in. This duality is everywhere in the poems, as are the conventionally treated ironic situations, the death of the young, the inefficacy of innocence, the self-destroying essence of sexual love.

All this is structural, but its effectiveness—as in the case of equilibrium-tension—depends on the texture, on the sense of irony which is woven into it.

Socratic irony, by which we come painfully to knowledge through ignorance, works through a number of the poems, notably "Necrological," where the good Friar stumbles his way through platitudes and stock responses for the questions implicit in the carnage he sees around him and comes thereby to a recognition of the inadequacy of his ready answers and then to a final identification with the dead, who, in the most terrible irony, are "solicited" with "sweet cries" by the "kites of Heaven." And working through all of the poems is what Wasserman [20] has called Schlegelian irony, the revelation of the poet's subjective self through the objectivity of his work.

This is no more true of Ransom's poetry than it is of any serious work, poetry or fiction, except that Ransom contrives (and the term here is not pejorative)—to invest his poems with an objectivity in such a way that we are able to see the contrivance function more clearly—perhaps the word is more dramatically—than we can with most writers. We can see him when he decides to step back from his subject, and we can watch him move in again; we know when, and he intends for us to see by what means, he becomes disengaged or disengages us the readers. We know at once when he wants to move himself into the poem; we sense his personal feelings in the closing of "Janet Waking" as strongly as they are spelled out in the closing lines of "The Equilibrists." But these feelings are betrayed as wel¹ in the cooler passages of all three poems by the very objectivity which the poet builds to keep the passions out of the picture.

Through all this there still operates the pervasive irony· of tone, the tension between sentiment inherent in the situation and the apparent inappropriateness of the language, whether it is the Latinate language of objectivity or the language of wit. He "combines an amusing texture," as George Williamson puts it, "with serious emotion." [21] He treats the potentially maudlin with a classical language, a classical detachment. Louis Rubin sees "The underlying mood of Ransom's poetry" as "terror and savagery masked by urbanity; the tension of a violent content described in bloodless language." [22] In the use of wit—in "Captain Carpenter," for instance, or even "Piazza Piece"—the amusing, almost comical pose balances the tendency of the subject to be overintent, to take itself too seriously, to be puffed up, pretentious.

This is the peril of many of the themes to which Ransom is drawn. Few poets would approach, with much hope of success, stories about a little girl whose pet chicken has died; about a woman whose lovely flowers have been cut down by a storm; about a little dead boy; about a dead girl whose geese miss her when she has gone. The poetry of Ransom is—more so even than the poetry of his companions in the New Criticism—informed by the attitude evident here, a strongly and consistently ironic view of the world. It invests the best of his work with credibility and with that strange quality of disengaged compassion which we have come to recognize as a part of his signature. There is love, naked but sufficiently distant, and there is grandeur and majesty, real and full of honor but crowned by wit: the detachment which Bradbury has called "the enabling act of poetry." [23] In the two poems which follow, perhaps as well as in any of Ransom's work, we can see the act of detachment as

31

the enabling act by which the poet reveals his subjective self in the carefully objective line.

JANET WAKING

Beautifully Janet slept
Till it was deeply morning. She woke then
And thought about her dainty-feathered hen,
To see how it had kept.

One kiss she gave her mother.
Only a small one gave she to her daddy
Who would have kissed each curl of his shining baby;
No kiss at all for her brother.

"Old Chucky, old Chucky!" she cried,
Running across the world upon the grass
To Chucky's house, and listening. But alas,
Her Chucky had died.

It was a transmogrifying bee
Came droning down on Chucky's old bald head
And sat and put the poison. It scarcely bled,
But how exceedingly

And purply did the knot
Swell with the venom and communicate
Its rigor! Now the poor comb stood up straight
But Chucky did not.

So there was Janet
Kneeling on the wet grass, crying her brown hen
(Translated far beyond the daughters of men)
To rise and walk upon it.

And weeping fast as she had breath
Janet implored us, "Wake her from her sleep!"

And would not be instructed in how deep
Was the forgetful kingdom of death.

DEAD BOY

The little cousin is dead, by foul subtraction,
A green bough from Virginia's aged tree,
And none of the county kin like the transaction,
Nor some of the world of outer dark, like me.

A boy not beautiful, nor good, nor clever,
A black cloud full of storms too hot for keeping,
A sword beneath his mother's heart—yet never
Woman bewept her babe as this is weeping.

A pig with a pasty face, so I had said,
Squealing for cookies, kinned by poor pretense
With a noble house. But the little man quite dead,
I see the forbears' antique lineaments.

The elder men have strode by the box of death
To the wide flag porch, and muttering low send round
The bruit of the day. O friendly waste of breath!
Their hearts are hurt with a deep dynastic wound.

He was pale and little, the foolish neighbors say;
The first-fruits, saith the Preacher, the Lord hath taken;
But this was the old tree's late branch wrenched away,
Grieving the sapless limbs, the shorn and shaken.

The "little cousin," as dangerous an opening as the "little
body" of John Whiteside's daughter, is removed to the right distance by the introduction of an apparently out-of-place term
with connotations far from the *ambiente* of the poem. "Foul
subtraction" suggests a transaction and carries the sense that
such dying, albeit unpleasant, is not outside the realm of the
day-to-day business of this world. It is a world, after all, which

cares little for the concerns of man. This is one of Ransom's most effective uses of Latinate terms with deliberate reference to the root meaning, a practice which allows him to speak with a precision not possible in the modern sense of the words and at the same time with a remarkable ambiguity.

He takes us to the deeper meaning, the almost lost meaning, of the word, which now to our ears acts as a connotation of the word, so that technical and objective as the terms are, they become in Ransom's line three-dimensional. "Subtraction" is a drawing from under; "transaction" is a carrying across. This last, especially since it is followed by the "world of outer dark," puts us in mind of the River Styx, and we are in a context at once more classical, more distant, and more noble than we were before.

The irony of the poem is not found primarily in the tension between the family's status and the observation that the boy was "a pig with a pasty face" nor in the pull between the seriousness of the subject and the tone of the language. It is at least half in the realization we must be drawn to that, if the boy had lived, the dynasty would probably not have survived with him. Antique, indeed, are the forbears' lineaments.

More often than not, the ironic view Ransom takes of the world, which gives rise to the equilibrium-forces in the poems, is itself born of Ransom's concern with the "dissociation of sensibility," Eliot's term applied by Warren to the poetry of Ransom a generation ago.[24]

Ransom tells us that very early in his life he had come to distrust abstraction. From this continuing and finally rationalized distrust has come much of the concreteness of his images, the reluctance to philosophize in the poems, and his advocacy of the ontological approach to criticism. We know that in Ransom's view abstraction brings man to nothing, addressing itself as it must to the mean, the typical. As the idea of a chair must include all chairs, it can describe no chair in particular. Ransom is interested in *particular* chairs, for it is the particular and concrete to which we react with feeling, that insinuates itself into our memories as part of an experience past, or that we see, touch, fall out of or bump into as part of an experience. For the senses the abstract chair does not exist. It is not a part of those particularities with which God has built the world, but instead is a part of man's attempt to dominate that world. It is useless to the poet.

Furthermore, it is dangerous to employ abstractions. We can learn so effectively to abstract, to generalize, to intellectualize, that we are no longer able to respond intuitively to the first experience; we give it over to the head, which makes fact always subject to abstract consideration and disintegrates the concrete and immediate thing there before us. Experience as contact with the world, through the senses, becomes impossible.

The mind which lives on abstraction and the mind which hunts out the concrete are working at cross-purposes; if they ever meet, it is in collision. Summing up Ransom's thinking, Louise Cowan puts it this way: "The inner content of his poetry derives . . . from the very core of human existence, which . . . is shaken by the two antithetical attitudes: the scientific and philosophic desire to possess and control and the religious and aesthetic urge to contemplate and love." [25] It has not been put better.

But however the conflict is seen, the body has—as Ransom might say—capitulated. Science, or the scientific myth, has given force and direction to abstraction as a way of life, and man has learned—has been urged—to intellectualize his passions.

If Ransom would have had it otherwise, he does not tell us that the head should not function but that it should not function as a thing unto itself, apart from the sensate flesh and dominant over it. It is the dissociation which Ransom abhors; ironically, that separation of parts which requires the balance we would not need if our parts were not apart. It is this which turns his mind to equilibria, to polarities.

In "Painted Head" he mourns the decapitation of man, who can no longer think and feel as one thing, can no longer hold a fact and its idea together, cannot decide whether he wants to exult in the world or manipulate it; man who is forever tripping over his own head:

35

By dark severance the apparition head
Smiles from the air a capital on no
Column or a Platonic perhaps head
On a canvas sky depending from nothing;

Stirs up an old illusion of grandeur
By tickling the instinct of heads to be
Absolute and to try decapitation
And to play truant from the body bush;

But too happy and beautiful for those sorts
Of head (homekeeping heads are happiest)
Discovers maybe thirty unwidowed years
Of not dishonoring the faithful stem;

Is nameless and has authored for the evil
Historian headhunters neither book
Nor state and is therefore distinct from tart
Heads with crowns and guilty gallery heads;

Wherefore the extravagant device of art
Unhousing by abstraction this once head
Was capital irony by a loving hand
That knew the no treason of a head like this;

Makes repentance in an unlovely head
For having vinegarly traduced the flesh
Till, the hurt flesh recusing, the hard egg
Is shrunken to its own deathlike surface;

And an image thus. The body bears the head
(So hardly one they terribly are two)
Feeds and obeys and unto please what end?
Not to the glory of tyrant head but to

The estate of body. Beauty is of body.
The flesh contouring shallowly on a head
Is a rock-garden needing body's love
And best bodiness to colorify

The big blue birds sitting and sea-shell flats
And caves, and on the iron acropolis
To spread the hyacinthine hair and rear
The olive garden for the nightingales.

Science is handmaiden to the arts, or better be, he says, then
shifts the metaphor to suggest a deeper relationship: the humanities give science its soul, without which science is a monster.

As large as Ransom's concern for the dehumanizing effect of
abstraction, growing partly out of that and manifesting itself in
every poem, woven through every texture, is the ironic view. It
is as natural to Ransom's mind, surely, as any fury. It is the voice
of the stoic, the quality of the poet, and he says so in a statement which comes close to being a personal *ars poetica*.

AGITATO MA NON TROPPO

This is what the man said,
Insisting, standing on his head.

Yes, I have come to grief,
It was not furtive like a thief,
And must not be blown up beyond belief.

They know I have no bittern by the lake
To cry it up and down the brake,
And nothing since has been like Dante's fury
For Beatrice who was not his to bury,
Except, if the young heart faltered, they may know
How Shelley's throbbing reed sang tremolo.

They say, "He puts a fix upon his mind,
And hears at bedside or in the moaning wind
The rumor of Death; yet he can't mount one tear
But stalks with holy calm beside the terrible bier."

Lest we wreck upon a reef,
I go according to another brief,
Against their killing blasts of grief.

My head, outposted promontoried chief,
Frowned, and elected me to the common grief,
By whose poor pities I'm shaken, but not as a leaf.

Here is grief understated; something on the poet's mind, told but muted, a story played out across a field at dusk, or woven into a tapestry. He is shaken, but not much. In the poem as in the man, in the rational humanist who dislikes equally the extreme show of pleasure or the blatant display of grief, this is the way it has to be. It is the world as Ransom would have it, and it is the world his characters dwell in.

Blue Birds and Grey Veils:
Symbolism and Suggestion

It is not surprising, since the Fugitives were withdrawn from the revolution in taste and technique led by Pound and Eliot, a revolution greatly influenced by the French symbolists, that Ransom did not become a symbolist poet. When Ransom shows us one thing to speak of another, he depends not so much upon the symbol as the metaphor.

There are a few words which recur so often in Ransom's poetry that the reader sometimes takes them to be part of a system of symbols, but in the case of substantives, in particular, this is not so. Many of the words suspected of being a part of such a system are in fact not intended to carry any special symbolic import at all: "skull," for instance, and "tall," which are words Ransom likes. And "trees," "birds," "leaves" and "grass." This is not to say that these words are meant to carry nothing beyond their definition. "Skull," as one would expect, reinforces the idea of mortality. "Tall" suggests nobility. They work together toward both these ideas as the "tall skull" in "The Equilibrists." "Trees" may suggest sometimes the fullness of life, of nature, as in the willows of "Vision by Sweetwater," but they more often represent "family," as in "Parting, without a Sequel," when the woman who has written a letter telling her lover good-bye goes for counsel to the tree which so clearly embodies the spirit of her father that she understands the rustling of the leaves as his voice speaking to her. It also represents family in the "Dead Boy," who was a late branch of the "old tree." The bird-cries in the hackberry trees of "Two In August" reflect the argument of the man and his wife, and the tree suggests the marriage, the home.

The "Druid trees" of "The Vanity of the Bright Boys" carry the suggestion of wisdom, as the vaunting oak does in "Parting, without a Sequel," but the Druid trees also clearly say "family," since the young man is looking for that, carrying in his head the royalty by fancy which is not in his blood by family.

The "Vaunting Oak" of that poem—and this also is extended from the quality of "family"—represents permanence, solidarity. If it happens that the appearance of solidarity is false, the irony only enriches the suggestion.

"Leaves" take their sense from the trees, as they are "susceptive/To the mad humors of the wind, and turn and flee/In panic round the stem on which they are captive" ("Vaunting Oak"). In "Of Margaret" a leaf is a "wafer body" falling from a tree; and the girl would mourn it as her own "first born." In all these the tree still is the family-base, or the father-mother family core, and the leaves are the individual and more "susceptive," weaker offspring.

In "Agitato ma non troppo," only this quality of susceptibility—especially to the mad humor which is grief—concerns the poet: "I'm shaken, but not as a leaf."

This is an extension of the more usual intent of the word, but it is comfortably within a range of implications—young, weak, fragile, unstable, impermanent, susceptive—which the word can call up.

So also the introduction of "birds" into a poem may suggest any of a wide range of qualities, the fullness, quickness of life as in "Blue Girls," when the blue birds walk upon the grass; in "Spectral Lovers," when the lovers' "quick fingers" flutter "like birds." The "timid lady bird" of "Lady Lost" suggests something not far from this, though here the suggestion is one of the richness of life, love perhaps, and beauty.

40

Knight [26] points out Ransom's use of birds as depository of the attitudes of the characters, as in "Two in August," when the birds on the tree seem to be echoing the couple's quarrel and also reflect the tumult within the man himself. As he cannot give up the sweet pridefulness of the position he has taken, or of his sense of righteousness, and still cannot abide being separated from his love, so he cannot tell whether the cries of the birds are "of heaven or hell."

Grass also has considerable use in Ransom's work. The birds in "Blue Girls," as we have noted, are seen walking across it. In "Janet Waking," the little girl goes "running across the world" upon it; in "Two in August," the man treads "the dim lawn." In all three of these poems, the actions stand simply for living on the earth, going about the business of living, whether for those lives the world is bright or dim. The geese in "Bells for John Whiteside's Daughter" are "like a snow cloud/Dripping their snow on the green grass." Significantly it is only the geese which walk upon that grass now; the girl is dead.

Ransom uses "head" to represent the intellect, reason. Sometimes it stands for morality, with the implication that the mind and soul cohabitate or perhaps are parts of the same thing. At any rate, we find the head to be the place not only of reason, as in "Painted Head," and control, restraint, as in "Agitato ma non troppo," but, for "The Equilibrists," the roost of the doves that come crying "Honor, Honor," stilling the passion of the lovers.

And "head" is usually a counterpiece to "body" (which stands for passion, physical love), or to the sentiments, intuition, spontaneity, which in the poems are not usually represented by anything concrete; they are either submerged or called by name. But it is this polarity between head as intellect on the one hand and body as intuitive or emotional response on the other which gives full meaning to the moment in "Necrological" where the friar, despairing that his reason, his detached observation of the carnage about him, might tell him what he wanted to know, what mattered, sat down "and bowed his head," and finally, with his intellect humbled, was able to come to a kind of epiphany, a kinship with the dead.

There are only these few substantives which are used in this way

41

frequently enough to deserve much discussion. Ransom does not expect them to do too much. It is when he brings in color that he works with a serious and almost systematic symbolic intent.

The colors he uses most are blue, white, red, and green, in that order. He stays nearly all the time though with either black or white, on one of the ends of the spectrum. Not surprisingly, there is method in this.

For that method we go to Ransom's use of polarity, because the colors are best considered not as discrete symbols, working alone, each to its own end, but as bands on a spectrum whose extremes are passion, anger, evil (red) and innocence, the playful and pure—if a sensual purity—(blues). As the solar spectrum runs from red to blues—red, orange, yellow, green, blue, indigo and violet—with green in the middle, so green in Ransom's poems often suggests the point of equilibrium between the extremes— peace, well-being or youth. In yellow, which is close to green, but toward the red end of that special spectrum light breaks into for Ranson, lies the sense of the peaceful, the inviting, but with a strong undertone of mystery, the unknown, almost the fore- boding.

Here, by way of recapitulation, are some specific examples of how the colors work.

Red is evil, passion and anger. Ransom's "Dog," the invader of the bull's harem, has "two red eyes," and even the sky is red, as "The heavens bleed."

The red of Captain Carpenter's heart is all passion and fury, and is even "red red." The rogue who cuts it out is something more than this, is driven by a less noble passion, is evil. Ransom makes him scarlet, a variety of red; like the Captain, but not the same.

In "Emily Hardcastle, Spinster," the dead woman is attended by the sisters "who are red-eyed, who are wroth."

Blue is innocence, playfulness and purity. The relative inno- cence of the woman's world in "Prelude to an Evening," the purity she protects, is suggested by the "blue bowls" whose water she keeps fresh. The "Man without Sense of Direction," who is lifeless, cold to the world, must love his lovely woman, whose head is rinsed in blue air, and Ralph, in "Morning," lies beside

Jane and with playful thoughts dancing over him like "imps" lets "his stare/penetrate dazedly into the blue air."

The clearest use of blue in this way comes in "Blue Girls," where the maidens are exhorted to be like the blue birds that— again—"go walking on the grass," that chatter on the air; to enjoy living, to gather their rosebuds and have fun. They will lose their youth and with it their illusions, will be like the lady with the terrible tongue, who has lost her "blue," her illusions, her zeal for life, and her innocence.

BLUE GIRLS

Twirling your blue skirts, travelling the sward
Under the towers of your seminary,
Go listen to your teachers old and contrary
Without believing a word.

Tie the white fillets then about your hair
And think no more of what will come to pass
Than bluebirds that go walking on the grass
And chattering on the air.

Practise your beauty, blue girls, before it fail;
And I will cry with my loud lips and publish
Beauty which all our power shall never establish,
It is so frail.

For I could tell you a story which is true;
I know a woman with a terrible tongue,
Blear eyes fallen from blue,
All her perfections tarnished—yet it is not long
Since she was lovelier than any of you.

Since green is peace, well-being and youth, the house of the Van Vroomans, from which we begin the "First Travels of Max," sits on a green slope, where it is in itself a symbol of peace and security.

The "Vaunting Oak" puts forth "green banners of peace," and the geese, in "Bells for John Whiteside's Daughter," used to run ahead of her on the green grass, where they dropped their feathers like snow. Ransom might have felt it necessary to point out the color of the "banners" in order to be sure that we understood the invisible side of the metaphor to be the leaves, but certainly he did not think it was necessary to tell us the color of the grass, simply for our information. It is green here because the girl was young and playful and it is being covered with white because she is dead.

Yellow is pleasant, restful, inviting, with an undertone of mystery, almost of foreboding. Quiescent is perhaps the best word, as it carries the hint of something which is asleep and may—or surely will—wake up.

In "Vaunting Oak," a flat where grow flowers of "yellow kinds" "had to be traversed" before the lovers could get to the tree. Here Ransom tells us that the girl had been "instructed well by much mortality." The color implies that she will soon be instructed of more, and she is. The tree which for her represents endurance, strength and stability, proves to be hollow.

Max, in his travels, comes upon a witch—who, significantly, is red—with a "bosom wide and yellow as butter." It is inviting, conventionally a place where man rests his head for consolation, but there is a frightening mystery about the bosom, a terror the little boy cannot quite grasp. "When I am a grown man," he cries, "I will come here/And cut your head off!"

The "Antique Harvesters," seeing how "declension looks from our land," seeing the decay of the old South, seeing the "meager hill of kernels" which is the harvest, looking forward with courage but misgiving, "assemble, dry, grey, spare,/And mild as yellow air." Surely the land is as beautiful and inviting as it is terrible.

Aside from these colors, Ransom uses black and white, plus grey (or ashy), and pale, in the way of symbols though the sense they carry is generally so conventional, so universally associated with the respective colors, that the use of the colors seems almost more descriptive than symbolic.

Black is the color of foreboding, the unknown, and the somber. The witch in "Ecologue" is black, as is the devil Captain Carpenter meets, and the "Spectral Lovers" rise out of the black ground.

White is the color sometimes of death, often of purity and of sensuality. A number of times these last two are taken together, where the sensuality is heightened by the purity, as in "The Equilibrists"; the unattainable body of the woman is a "white field ready for love." The woman in "Spectral Lovers" is a city of "white peace." "In Process of a Noble Alliance" (1963 edition) has the bride in "funeral white," a fusion again of purity and sensuality, this time with the additional sense of death, which the color white also represents. This convention Ransom uses a number of times, as in "Necrological," where white corpses are scattered about a white field.

Grey hints of hopelessness, isolation and related feelings, and often of death, especially when the poet is treating not actual death, but death in effect. It is opposite to the greens and blues of full life, excitement and hope. Death appears to the young lady of "Piazza Piece" as a "grey man." In "Antique Harvesters," a poem about the decline of the South, grey appears three times. Color as symbol is particularly important in "Judith of Bethulia."

Beautiful as the flying legend of some leopard
She had not chosen yet her captain, nor Prince
Depositary to her flesh, and our defense;
A wandering beauty is a blade out of its scabbard.
You know how dangerous, gentlemen of threescore?
May you know it yet ten more.

Nor by process of veiling she grew less fabulous.
Grey or blue veils, we were desperate to study
The invincible emanations of her white body,
And the winds at her ordered raiment were ominous.
Might she walk in the market, sit in the council of soldiers?
Only of the extreme elders.

But a rare chance was the girl's then, when the Invader
Trumpeted from the South, and rumbled from the North,
Beleaguered the city from four quarters of the earth,
Our soldiery to craven and sick to aid her—

Where were the arms could countervail this horde?
Her beauty was the sword.

She sat with the elders, and proved on their blear visage
How bright was the weapon unrusted in her keeping,
While he lay surfeiting on their harvest heaping
Wasting the husbandry of their rarest vintage—
And dreaming of the broad-breasted dames for concubine?
These floated on his wine.

He was lapped with bay-leaves, and grass and fumiter weed,
And from under the wine-film encountered his mortal vision,
For even within his tent she accomplished his derision,
Loosing one veil and another, she stood unafraid;
So he perished. Nor brushed her with even so much as a daisy?
She found his destruction easy.

The heathen have all perished. The victory was furnished.
We smote them hiding in vineyards, barns, annexes,
And now their white bones clutter the holes of foxes,
And the chieftain's head, with grinning sockets, and varnished—
Is it hung on the sky with a hideous epitaphy?
No, the woman keeps the trophy.

May God send unto our virtuous lady her Prince!
It is stated she went reluctant to that orgy,
Yet a madness fevers our young men, and not the clergy
Nor the elders have turned them unto modesty since.
Inflamed by the thought of her nakedness with desire?
Yes, and chilled with fear and despair.

Judith hides her white body from the lusting young men behind "grey or blue veils." Blue because she is virginal and innocent, pure of body if not of heart. The white of her body is the
white of untouched sensuality and desire. The grey veils tell of
the death she brings to Holofernes and the intimations of death
which the young men have afterwards.

46

Ransom has remarked, by the way, on his treatment of the women in his poems, that it is a "gallant" treatment, and this is beautifully so. Sometimes it is strangely so, since the women in his poems are in several cases stronger, more aggressive than the men and know better what they are about. If they are not in control we feel they ought to be. It is true here, and there is something of it in "Conrad," in "Old Mansion," "Prelude to an Evening," and even in "Captain Carpenter" and "First Travels of Max."

Paleness is used to convey weakness, negation, withdrawal from life. It is at the opposite pole, as we would expect it to be, from the bright colors, regardless of the quality of the brightness: red, green, blue or white.

"Hilda," rejecting her suitor, is a "pale girl," and the memories which haunt the man like ghosts come to him as "blanched lepers." The woman in "Parting without a Sequel," also denying her lover, is "too pale for tears/Observing the ruin of her younger years," and is her father's "wan daughter."

Knight [27] notes the use of pallid whiteness in Ransom's poems as distinct from vibrant whiteness, including it among the "pale symbols," pointing out that "the 'white dawn' of 'Parting at Dawn' must . . . be a pallid color, for it is the time for the separation of lovers who apparently will meet no more, the time when there is a 'cold glitter of light.' "

The other colors Ransom makes use of are bronze or tawny, brown, and pink. The first is essentially descriptive and is used in association with an antique richness or the fullness of maturity, as for instance the tawny leaves and bronze harvest of "Antique Harvesters." Brown is a color Ransom apparently associates with animals: the bird in "Lady Lost" is brown, and in "Janet Waking" it is a brown hen transmogrified by the bee.

Pink, the one time it is used in Ransom's 1969 Selection, is significantly just what pink is: a weak red. When the red bull, a furious and deadly beast, is set against the dog, we remember that the smaller animal's yap is his "pink paradigm."

Aside from the uses outlined here, Ransom employs almost all of these same colors in a purely descriptive manner when it serves his purposes with no symbolic import, except what may always

47

be inseparable from the color. A house of red brick can be simply a house of red brick.

Now and then Ransom gives a character in his poems a name which reveals something the poet wants us to know about the character. This is not symbolism, because the character is an important figure in his own right and will not be reduced to a symbol; it is not allegory because the character does not stand for an abstract quality, but rather embodies the quality, which interests us here only in terms of *this* character. Still the name-giving harks back to the morality play or more exactly to the names which the Puritans, in wishful thinking at least, gave to their children.

The name of "Emily Hardcastle, Spinster," explicates itself in terms of the poem. Ransom has said that he had not only Thomas Hardy (to whom the poem was dedicated in earlier versions) but also Joseph Conrad in mind in naming "Conrad Sits in Twilight" (now "Master's in the Garden Again"); yet the fact that the meaning carried by the name is "wise-in-counsel" gives pause to the reader who happens to have that fragment of information.

The wounded soldier in "Puncture"—a Christ-figure ("But they have stuck your side" . . . "I never knew your mortal blood/Had wasted for my sake") but no Christ—is given the name of Grimes to represent his actual humanity, his origins in this world—his undivinity, as Ransom might have said it.

We recognize "Captain Carpenter" at once as a Quixote, but cannot miss the suggestion of Our Captain, the Carpenter, who went armed with faith and virtue to rid the world of evil and has had devils and their wives to contend with.

These are some of the things Ransom makes use of to say more than he says, to enrich the undermeanings and make the lines reverberate with suggestion. He uses them well, and it is important that he does not use them too much.

These are major elements in his poetry, but perhaps the most vital has not been mentioned yet in the context of the symbol: unconsummated passion, the stuff of which Ransom structures most of his polarities, abstraction though it is, is itself a symbol of that abstraction which to Ransom was most terrible and almost visibly present, almost a living enemy. This is the dissociation of sensibility, that theme which pervades most of Ransom's work and informs his use of contrast and metaphor, his understanding of color. And so the names for the poles which hold our parts apart—heat and cold, bright and dull, flames and ice, chills and fevers, all standing for the intellect and passions, the head and the body—are central to much of Ransom's poetry, as passion too much thought about and so undone, sensibility split in two. This is the schizophrenia from which the majority of Ransom's people suffer. But if the people are inventions of Ransom's the dichotomy is not. The reader knows it from outside the poems and sees that Emily Hardcastle finally is a symbol of the reader and that her colors are the colors we wear. All of these elements are working together in "Spectral Lovers":

By night they haunted a thicket of April mist,
Out of that black ground suddenly come to birth,
Else angels lost in each other and fallen on earth.
Lovers they knew they were, but why unclasped unkissed?
Why should two lovers be frozen apart in fear?
And yet they were, they were.

Over the shredding of an April blossom
Scarcely her fingers touched him, quick with care,
Yet of evasions even she made a snare.
The heart was bold that clanged within her bosom,
The moment perfect, the time stopped for them,
Still her face turned from him.

Strong were the batteries of the April night
And the stealthy emanations of the field;
Should the walls of her prison undefended yield
And open her treasure to the first clamorous knight?
"This is the mad moon, and shall I surrender all?
If he but ask it I shall."

And gesturing largely to the moon of Easter,
Mincing his steps and swishing the jubilant grass,
Beheading some field-flowers that had come to pass,

He had reduced his tributaries faster
Had not considerations pinched his heart
Unfitly for his art.

"Do I reel with the sap of April like a drunkard?
Blessed is he that taketh this richest of cities;
But it is so stainless the sack were a thousand pities.
This is that marble fortress not to be conquered,
Lest its white peace in the black flame turn to tinder
And an unutterable cinder."

They passed me once in April, in the mist.
No other season is it when one walks and discovers
Two tall and wandering, like spectral lovers,
White in the season's moon-gold and amethyst,
Who touch quick fingers fluttering like a bird
Whose songs shall never be heard.

It is interesting to note that here again the woman is the stronger figure, or at least the aggressive one. Her heart is bold; she lets their fingers just touch. Indeed her evasions are snares. The man does not appear to be an experienced lover, but she, by woman's instinct if not by practice, clearly knows what she is about. She does everything she can to get him to seduce her, but he walks with mincing steps and gives his violence to the grass, deflowering the field.

We see at last, in the fourth stanza, that Ransom has given us another treatment of the theme of dissociation. The boy's head has taken him over. He is intellectualizing and we can hear him go about it. With almost everyone, that is what is the matter.

The Thing Behind the Thing:
Metaphor and Other
Sideway Glances

Every poet makes use of metaphor—and I use the word here to include the weaker comparisons, simile and metonomy—towards a number of ends: to heighten emotional intensity, to emphasize and elucidate an idea, to carry an image, as an aid to irony and to make the poem a sensual experience by rendering the intangible concrete. In Ransom's poetry, metaphor does all this, the last with a special meaning to the poet, and serves another end which is peculiar to Ransom—the raising and lowering of a creature's state according to Ransom's own scale of being.

There is nearly always a heightened emotional import when metaphor is introduced, because the range of associations drawn on is wider, because the image which a metaphor generally involves acts on our senses and because the reader is involved in making real for himself the implied identity of the two sides. There would be little use in citing such instances in Ransom's poetry to show this or his use of the metaphor in the elucidation of an idea, since that, in part, is the nature of comparison. These are mentioned only as a reminder that in addition to other functions served by many metaphors in Ransom's poetry, they are at the same time functioning according to their conventional ends.

It is also in the natural use of metaphor that it may translate the intangible into the concrete. This is where the image usually comes from. But Ransom is not simply building pictures and attracting attention by tickling the senses. His interest is deeper than this. It follows from his aversion to abstraction that he should find special meaning in the particular, the touchable. For Ransom man's sanity depends upon his contact with the concrete and identifiable things of the world, on the recognition and the celebration of them. As Knight has put it,[28] "Ransom . . . uses metaphors in order to supply a generous and pleasurable sampling of 'the World's Body,' the thing which poetry by his definition seeks to recapture."

Death we have seen as an old man in a dustcoat. Death is also a Grizzled Baron—elucidation, certainly, but primarily an incarnation: the idea taken flesh. Memories are "blanched lepers." Love is honey on the lover's lips.

And Ransom uses metaphor to emphasize an irony. The "Man without Sense of Direction," without purpose or decision or much manhood, clearly no Greek hero, writhes in his private torment "like an antique man of bronze/That is beaten by furies visible." Before their "Armageddon," Christ is called, conventionally, a lamb. Satan is the wolf. But it is Christ, not Satan, who is eager for the bloodshed.

Ransom's most interesting use of metaphor is his alone and is one of the distinguishing characteristics of his poetry. Several writers have noted his practice of employing metaphors which domesticate the exotic and render mundane the noble, as in the closing of "Winter Remembered," when the speaker, remembering a separation from his sweetheart, tells her:

> Dear love, these fingers that had known your touch,
> And tied our separate forces first together,
> Were ten poor idiot fingers not worth much,
> Ten frozen parsnips hanging in the weather.

If the first three lines might have come from the best of the seventeenth century, the final line is as modern in every meaning of the word as Eliot's "ragged claws" or Jarrell's cockpit.

But what has not been pointed out is the whole pattern of which this domesticating is only half. It is found in the Bible, though this is not to say that Ransom found it there.

Thus saith the Lord God; Remove the diadem, and take off the crown: this shall not be the same; exalt him that is low, and abase him that is high.

Ezekiel 21:26

Abasement is the direction taken by many of Ransom's metaphors. People are rendered as animals or insects, vegetables or machines, but almost always these are people who were elevated, or at least sympathetic, to begin with.

We meet the husband who is a "wolf/Dragging his infected wound homeward" ("Prelude to an Evening"); the lover whose fingers, at one time sensate and loving, had become "Ten frozen parsnips" ("Winter Remembered"); the young man who looks "absurd" in his "tight black coat like a sleazy beetle" ("The Vanity of the Bright Boys"). In "Old Man Pondered" in the 1963 edition, there is the man who has so successfully shut himself off from human feelings that his eye is not an eye but an "optic gate." In the context of the lines we imagine a drawbridge, chains and gears, but no flesh. The man is a thing other than human, and less than human. There is the crusader ("Captain Carpenter") who has his legs broken for him by a rogue, letting the captain "roll and stick like any tub."

In "Vision by Sweetwater," the girls who will at last represent Hellenic maidens are shown as pleasant but less than noble creatures, "light as wrens/If there were a little colony all hens." In "Two Gentlemen in Bonds," the title poem from the earlier book (a poem which Ransom has not included in the later selections), the gentlemen who are "pink and slippered . . . dance like locusts." The "Dead Boy" in his poem is a scion of aristocracy, last of a proud line, but also is "a pig with a pasty face."

The wife of "Two in August," upset over the quarrel with her husband and angry, circuits "the dark rooms like a string of amber." It is impossible to miss the suggestion of the insect and incidentally to see the idea of the tree still working here behind the amber as the family, the home.

People of good position or people Ransom likes are apt to be left, when the poem is done, with less than they had to begin with. But it happens also the other way. The "Vaunting Oak," which we know is less than it appears to be, is turned by Ransom into more than it is. He personifies it and in a kaleidoscopic confusion of metaphors has it giving birth to its leaves until, "delivered of his pangs" (a startling oxymoron, even for Ransom), he puts forth "profuse his green banners of peace" (hearkening back to the tower, which was the figure for the tree in the first line of the poem) and testifies to her "with innumerable tongues." There is a magnificance in all this, even if it comes as a little flamboyant to have the leaves as children a-borning, then banners, then tongues of a tree which was a tower to begin with. The tree, anyway, has moved up in the world.

In the 1963 edition, Grimes, the dirty old soldier, was a "fortress." The "Old Man Pondered," whose poem does not appear in the 1969 edition, was also apparently some kind of fortress, but now we have to think of *A Mighty Fortress Is My God*. On the field of battle, a fortress is the most desired of all things, and Grimes as a fortress was exalted and more than a man.

Referring again to "Master's in the Garden Again" and "Of Margaret," we see an expanded role in one falling leaf as a lost child and as a "first born." A cow is a "lady" and the dog barking ineffectually is like "a numerous army" in "Dog."

We meet the "Man without Sense of Direction," who, engaged in nothing that matters, is yet likened to the bronze hero, fighting those herculean battles the gods watch.

Those who don't have much to be said for them, Ransom lifts up. The point is that we are still dealing with the idea of equilibrium. Exalting the low and abasing the high, Ransom keeps his forces balanced, keeps both ends of all his seesaws off the ground at once and so holds the tension.

Now and then he carries his metaphor long enough, and we are allowed to look at it from enough angles, so that it becomes more than just a metaphor. We find ourselves in the middle of what we still manage to call a conceit. Ransom has fashioned some fine examples, some that any of his seventeenth-century counterparts would have been pleased to have written.

From "Old Man Pondered" (1963 edition):

> Many a bright-barbed hate
> Burning had smote against the optic gate
> To enter and destroy. But the quick gears
> Blinked shut the aperture. Else those grim leers
> Had won to the inner chamber where sat Hope
> To spin and pray . . .
>
> . . . And he must guard as well
> Against alluring love, whose mild engine
> Was perilous too for the lone sitter-in,
> So hard consented to her little cell;
> The tenderest looks vainly upon him fell.
>
> . . . lest one light arrow

The rock-garden metaphor in "Painted Head" is one of Ransom's most effective conceits.

The metaphor with which "Dead Boy" opens—the boy as a "green bough" and his family, "Virginia's aged tree"—is picked up again in the last stanza and held through three turns of the figure ("the first-fruits . . . the old tree's late branch wrenched away . . . Grieving the sapless limbs, the shorn and shaken").

A lady-as-besieged-city metaphor, clearly an echo of Donne, appears in stanza three of "Spectral Lovers," is carried for three lines, and then is picked up again in stanza five.

The dominant conceit figure in "The Equilibrists" is the woman as a medieval battlefield: her head is an "officious tower"; her body, "a white field ready for love." Her sexuality is lilies "beseeching him to take,/If he would pluck and wear them, bruise and break." The words of honor that keep him back are "swords." This is certainly the best-known and best-sustained conceit in Ransom's poetry.

It is interesting, in passing, to compare the attitude of Hilda towards Death, which was apparently ignoring her, with the attitude of the girl in "Piazza Piece," whom Death tried vigorously to seduce. In both cases the equilibrium stress comes in the *yes* given to *no* and the *no* given to *yes*. In Ransom's poems it is rare that two people want the same thing at the same time.

It has been said that a poet's work is a continuing search for the right metaphor; that when he finds it, the poem is all but finished. That is doubly true where the poem and the metaphor have the same boundaries, as frequently a metaphor is sustained by Ransom until it takes the whole poem, or, perhaps better said, the poem *is* the metaphor. Then the poem moves very close to allegory and would be that if the metaphors were consistently submerged and if we had people or animals representing ideas, which is what we expect of allegory. In these poems we usually have things representing ideas, but there are also things—ships or houses—representing people; and there are events—the falling of leaves, a venture into the woods—representing events. "Painted Head," belongs to this group. So do "Of Margaret," "Good Ships," "Emily Hardcastle, Spinster," and "In Process of a Noble Alliance." The poem-as-metaphor is a forte of Ransom's, and a number of such poems well done is no mean achievement. "Good Ships" and "In Process of a Noble Alliance" work particularly well in a few lines.

GOOD SHIPS

Fleet ships encountering on the high seas
Who speak, and then unto the vast diverge,
Two hailed each other, poised on the loud surge
Of one of Mrs. Grundy's Tuesday teas,
Nor trimmed one sail to baffle the driving breeze.
A macaroon absorbed all her emotion;
His hue was ruddy but an effect of ocean;
They exchanged the nautical technicalities.

It was only a nothing or so until they parted.
Away they went, most certainly bound for port,
So seaworthy one felt they could not sink;

Still there was a tremor shook them, I should think,
Beautiful timbers fit for storm and sport
And unto miserly merchant hulks converted.

IN PROCESS OF A NOBLE ALLIANCE

Reduce this lady unto marble quickly,
Ray her beauty on a glassy plate,
Rhyme her youth as fast as the granite,
Take her where she trembles and do not wait,
For now in funeral white they lead her
And crown her queen of the House of No Love:
A dirge then for her beauty, musicians!
Not harping the springe that catches the dove.

The metaphor in the second of the poems (which Ransom did not include in the 1969 edition) is a wedding rendered as a funeral. It is an emphatically inauspicious marriage because it is not a fusion in love but an "alliance" (perhaps it is not unfair to recall that the title of the poem when it first appeared in *Chills and Fevers* was "In Process of the Nuptials of the Duke"; we have to remember Browning's speaker and his own ill-fated duchess). Conventionally—it is a convention recognized repeatedly in Ransom's poems—the only person to take a lady without love, to lay her down and possess her simply for that, should be Death, the gentleman in the dustcoat, the Grizzled Baron. So the maiden we see here being readied for a wedding where there is no love is going to what seems to be, and might as well be, her funeral.

Another poem which appeared in *Chills and Fever,* but which was not included in the *Selected Poems* is "Triumph." Ransom was probably right to leave it where it was—he is an excellent judge of his own work—and the poem is mentioned here only because the opening stanza, although the rest of the poem does not measure up to it, is an impressive example of how the first side of a metaphor is set up, and with what sweep Ransom, not at all unlike Donne in these lines, moves into a poem to establish his metaphor. Still, if the poem does carry something of Donne

57

(and Pope, too) about it, it is assuredly Ransom. It leads into a love poem:

> Athens, a fragile kingdom by the foam,
> Assumed the stranger's yoke; but then behold how meek
> Those unbred Caesars grew, who spent their fruits of Rome
> Forever after, trying to be Greek.

This is an early poem, and if it is less than perfect in the stanzas that follow, the failure is in the language, not in the elaboration of the metaphor:

> I too shook out my locks like one born royal;
> For she dissolved in tears, and said my barbarous name,
> And took my oath, she was so piteous and loyal:
> Vote the young Caesar triumph, spread his fame!

> But oh, I find my captive was not caught.
> It was her empty house that fell before my legions;
> Of where her soul inhabits I have conquered naught;
> It is so far from these my Roman regions!

If the language is more effective in later poems, the metaphor is already at the poet's service.

One of the most effective means to achieve ambiguity, the least understood and the most maligned, is the use of the homonym, the word with two or more meanings: the pun.

Few since Shakespeare have had as much fun with word-play as Ransom has had. He uses it to excite the mind with echoes of related meanings, to intensify and sometimes elucidate the poem with ironic overtones, and to deepen the poem with secondary implications—especially sexual.

In the autumn, when nature seems to be dying, the earth is called *substant*. It is enduring, substantial; and it stands beneath us, our support.

In "Piazza Piece," the man in a dustcoat is of course a man in a coat of dust, and the wife of Satan determines that "Captain Carpenter" shall bear no more arms in more ways than one. In

"Prelude to an Evening," the speaker refers to lovemaking when he says, in the tenth stanza, "I would have us magnificent at my coming;/two souls tight-clasped."

Occasionally the difference between a word's contemporary and its root meaning is the basis for a punlike ambiguity: in "Old Man Pondered," the "sideway watery dog's glances" the young man gives his love are left "untold"; that is, both uncounted and unexplained.

The unhappy husband in "Two in August" finds that "the night-mastered birds were crying/With fear upon their tongues, no singing nor flying/Which are their lovely *attitudes* by dawn" (my italics). In other words, the lovely way of looking at the world, and also their lovely *skills,* which is the original meaning of the word, and which works here to effect a considerable enrichment of the line. I suspect that this is the meaning Ransom had first in mind.

"Reduce," the first word of the poem in "In Process of a Noble Alliance," is heavy with meaning. We think of *taking oxygen away,* of *distilling a thing to its essence,* of *simplifying,* or (to go, as Ransom likes to go, to the Latin root meaning) of *leading back* to the beginning—dust to dust. The literal intent is "make an image of."

Whatever name we choose to give the various means of identification and comparison, whatever end we see as their primary function, the fact that matters when we read is that few poets, if any, have learned to get as much out of so few words as Ransom consistently does. Almost every line of his poems is, on the literal level first, credible and understandable. If this were not true, no depth would excuse it. But the surface is there. We can walk upon the grass. And underneath it, like buried treasure, are the suggestions, the implications, the richness of irony and the hidden sides of the symbol and metaphor.

And over it all, like the blue ogive of the firmament, is the polarity of statement. This is the sound and the shape of Ransom's poetry, where it comes from.

Some Other Poems

NECROLOGICAL (The poem is found on pages 8–9.)

The friar is the man who intellectualizes his responses, who "figures out" the meaning of the life from which he has removed himself. It is easy to answer the insoluble problems with empty platitudes. This is the friar's way as he brings his head to make sense of the dead bodies around him: "the brother reasoned that . . . flesh fails." *Brother* is what he will finally become.

With the mistress, the monk is brought up against everything in the world of the flesh that might shake his faith in his cold metaphysic. That dark and real world outside the monastery of his mind is caving in on him, and a part of that is love as he has not understood it.

Finally the monk begins to become involved, to creep out from under the ruins of the monastery of his mind and make contact with the world. It is a strange experience for him, but the suggestion is that the sensual experience of the world—"He fingered it well, and it was cunningly made"—is not an unpleasant one.

There is confusion at last—"As under a riddle"—but it is not now an intellectual confusion. The friar is being initiated into the world of the senses, the concrete. He has become brother, and more. He identifies with the dead ones who, ironically, are being lured into heaven. It is as if they, by their flesh and its experience, have become heir to a heaven the friar has not guessed and probably can never know.

VISION BY SWEETWATER

Go and ask Robin to bring the girls over
To Sweetwater, said my Aunt; and that was why
It was like a dream of ladies sweeping by
The willows, clouds, deep meadowgrass, and river.

Robin's sisters and my Aunt's lily daughter
Laughed and talked, and tinkled light as wrens
If there were a little colony all hens
To go walking by the steep turn of Sweetwater.

Let them alone, dear Aunt, just for one minute
Till I go fishing in the dark of my mind:
Where have I seen before, against the wind,
These bright virgins, robed and bare of bonnet,

Flowing with music of their strange quick tongue
And adventuring with delicate paces by the stream,—
Myself a child, old suddenly at the scream
From one of the white throats which it hid among?

What appears on casual reading to be a fantasy, a daydream that turns suddenly into a nightmare, is more than that. What is moving under the surface sometimes comes so close to the top that we almost make out a shape, but it is a vague shape, and we are apt to leave the poem not quite sure the poet is getting at very much.

There is certainly a feeling of fantasy, but through that feeling Ransom gets to a moment of revelation—not a big thing, perhaps, and the reader may wonder, if he is not aware of how the moment plays against all of Ransom's poetry, whether it is worth the trouble.

The girls beside the river, the willows, clouds and grass draw gradually to the speaker's mind an old knowledge; he feels he has seen all this before, and he fishes for the memory beneath the feeling. It comes to him finally, out of a past he could not remember, a kind of racial memory, or out of the school books from his childhood, or both, that what he sees here is the setting for a Greek tragedy. Only one thing is lacking, and that comes with the scream from one of the girls. The scene is complete. The scream was necessary; the stage was waiting for it. Without it nothing Greek could be perfect.

In the third line we are warned that the actual girls are not the ones seen by the speaker; he is lost in some sort of dream, maybe nostalgia. The fancy comes out of the fact. Then in the second stanza we are warned further that something terrible might happen, or anyway could, as the "little colony all hens" goes walking near the "steep turn." It is interesting to note, in passing, that the etymology of *hen* takes us back to *canticle* or *chant,* which suggests the chorus of a Greek tragedy.

The "strange quick tongue" of the last stanza lets us know that the recognition, when it comes, will not be of anything local or even English. Then suddenly the speaker knows that what has been haunting him is the sense of the tragic and specifically the tragic as the Greek mind understood it. The scream resolves it, and as he identifies the ghost and gets rid of it in knowledge there is a catharsis of sorts.

What is not definite and doesn't need to be is whether one of the girls actually did scream, falling maybe into the steep turn of the river, for which we are prepared, thereby making the vision complete, or whether the imagination of the speaker completed its own vision, creating the scream, as it were, offstage. This I suspect is closer to the author's intention, both because of the poem's title and because it would require less melodrama.

What is also not definite and is more intriguing is the sense of the next-to-last line. Are we to think that the speaker is remembering a scream he heard as a child and which made him old in knowledge or that the present scream—real or imagined—has jerked him back from reveries of his childhood into his actual age? Either or neither. The *experience* is Greek; the tone, especially at the close, is steady, stoic. *This is how it is,* the poet has told us, *in the Greek mind. This is the act completed.* We remember, because we are Greek.

HERE LIES A LADY

Here lies a lady of beauty and high degree,
Of chills and fever she died, of fever and chills,
The delight of her husband, an aunt, and infant of three
And medicos marveling sweetly on her ills.

First she was hot, and her brightest eyes would blaze
And the speed of her flying fingers shook their heads.
What was she making? God knows; she sat in those days
With her newest gowns all torn, or snipt into shreds.

But that would pass, and the fire of her cheeks decline
Till she lay dishonored and wan like a rose overblown,
And would not open her eyes, to kisses, to wine;
The sixth of which states was final. The cold came down.

Fair ladies, long may you bloom, and sweetly may thole!
She was part lucky. With flowers and lace and mourning,
With love and bravado, we bade God rest her soul
After six quick turns of quaking, six of burning.

Here is another of the poems concerned with dissociation of sensibility. The lady is dying of it. She swings from heat to cold to heat again, from frenzy to frigidity, until, like a wire bent back and forth too long, she snaps. Notice that in the burning she was confident, busy making nothing, but sure of herself. This is the manic state. The fact that she turned out nothing but "shreds" defines her failure for us. There is no integrity; there is no whole self. It is the woman who has fallen to scraps of laces.

64

The third stanza is an almost clinical description of depression. The confidence goes off with the heat. It is consistent with Ransom that his metaphor for the woman, who to start with was elevated to a "high degree," lowers her to the condition of a vegetable, a "thin stalk" (1963 version) or a "dishonored rose" (1969 version).

It is difficult to resist taking "high degree" as a reference to a Ph.D., especially since the highly educated woman is often so susceptible to the kind of battle between her intellect and her passions that can lead to dissociation. It would probably be prudent, though, to be guided by Ransom's fondness for making his people lords and ladies and not make too much of that suggestion.

The "flowers and lace and mourning," carrying the assumption that the lace here is intact, speaks of an integrity of form and hints that finally in her death the woman was made whole. Her tug-of-war was over. And was she not lucky?

"Thole" is not used for show alone; there is remarkably little affectation in Ransom, but there is some posing for purpose: whimsy, irony, distance. Here it is for all three, but in large measure it is simply for economy: "thole" means both *struggle* and *endure*. Both meanings are important here and there isn't room for them. The word does yeoman duty. But beyond its use for whimsy, irony, distance and the advantage of distance, I suspect that Ransom would have told us a better reason for using the word: I suspect he would have told us that he liked the way it sounded.

FIRST TRAVELS OF MAX

In that old house of many generations
The best of the VanVroomans was the youngest.
But even Max, in a chevroned sailor's blouse
And tawny curls far from subdued to the cap,
Had slapped old Katie and removed himself
From games for children; that was because they told
Him never never to set a naughty foot
Into Fool's Forest, where the devil dwelt.

"Become Saint Michael's sword!" said Max to the stick,
And to the stone, "Be a forty-four revolver!"
Then Max was glad that he had armed so wisely
As darker grew the wood, and shrill with silence.
All good fairies were helpless here; at night
Whipped in an inch of their lives; weeping, forbidden
To play with strange scared truant little boys
Who didn't belong there. Snakes were allowed there
And lizards and adders—people of age and evil
That lay on their bellies and whispered—no bird nor rabbit.
There were more rotten trees than there were sound ones.
In that wood timber was degenerate
And rotted almost faster than it grew.
There were no flowers nor apples. Too much age.
The only innocent thing was really Max,
And even he had beat his little sisters.

The black tarn rose up almost in his face.
It was as black and sudden as the pit
The Adversary digs in the bowels of earth;
Bubbles were on it, breath of the black beast
(Formed like a spider, white bag for entrails)
Who took that sort of blackness to inhabit
And dangle after bad men in Fool's Forest.
"Must they be bad?" said casuistical Max.
"Mightn't a good boy who stopped saying his prayers
Be allowed to slip into the spider's fingers?"
Max raised his sword—but what can swords do
Against the Prince of the Dark? Max sheathed his point
And crept around the pool.
There in the middle of the wood was the Red Witch.
Max half expected her. He never imagined
A witch's house that would be red and dirty,
Or a witch's bosom wide and yellow as butter,
Or one that combed so many obscene things
From her black hair into her scarlet lap;
He never believed there would attempt to sing
The one that taught the rats to squeal and Bashan's
Bull to bellow.

"Littlest and last Van Vrooman, do you come too?"
She knew him, it appeared, would know him better,
The scarlet hulk of hell with a fat bosom
Pirouetting at the bottom of the forest.
Certainly Max had come, but he was going;
Unequal contests never being commanded
On young knights only armed in innocence.
"When I am a grown man I will come here
And cut your head off!" That was very well.
And no true heart beating in Christendom
Could have said more, but that for the present would do.

Max went straight home, and nothing chilled him more
Than the company kept him by the witch's laugh
And the witch's song, and the creeping of his flesh.

Max is more firmly domiciliated.
A great house is Van Vrooman, a green slope
South to the sun do the great ones inhabit,
And a few children play on the lawn with the nurse.
Max has returned to his play, and you may find him,
His famous curls unsmoothed, if you will call
Where the Van Vroomans live; the tribe Van Vrooman
Live there at least when any are at home.

This one is a poem of initiation, loss of innocence. Little Max
leaves the light and ordered security of his home to venture into
Fool's Forest, and comes back wiser than he was. He might be
taken for Captain Carpenter as a child, who tries to make good,
years later, his threat to go back and cut the witch's head off.

Max, youngest and, as tradition in the family would have it,
best of the Van Vrooman clan (Van Vrooman is a slight corrup-
tion of the Dutch for "True Man") was, even so, a rebellious sort,
which we should have guessed, even before he slapped his nurse,
when the poet is careful to point out how his curls will not be
"subdued to the cap." This time he is rebelling because he has
been told to stay in his own world, not to ask questions and
not to go into worlds he is not prepared for.

The poem works well all the way through on the literal level, if we allow Max to exaggerate a little about what he sees in the forest, but there is a metaphorical level not far under the surface. Max experiences an awakening which is at the same time intellectual—primarily this—and sexual.

He goes forth confident, as anyone is apt to who has never been put down very hard, whose world has turned always to his pleasure. This had been Max's world. He was not only wealthy; he was the youngest child. He still imagined that things would be as they ought to be; that here, as at home, the world would not be far from what he commanded. This, together with the natural ability of a young boy to believe his fancies, turns the stone to a revolver and the stick to a sword. It is interesting that the sword is Saint Michael's; Max apparently is feeling already that he has a mission, a vengeance to wreak.

Identifying himself with Michael (which means "One who is like God"), Max identifies himself also with the fairies (the angels of children), who are "whipped in an inch of their lives; weeping, forbidden/ To play with strange scared truant little boys." We cannot imagine that Max was ever beaten at all, but he surely feels that he has been put upon most cruelly and that he was forbidden to play with the other children.

Snakes (the first hint of sexual knowledge) and other crawling things are waiting on him in the darkness of the forest, but no symbols of innocence, no bird and no rabbit. The suggestion of sexual knowledge in the snake is confirmed by the picture of Eden: "There were no flowers nor apples. Too much age." It is an Eden ruined, decayed.

The black tarn, the pool that seems to rise up to meet him, shifts us from Genesis to Dante. Max becomes a sojourner through the inferno, with no guide. Then quickly he is the good Calvinist again. He is afraid the devil will have him for his small sins, and he prepares to do battle, until, like any Calvinist worthy of the name, he realizes the futility of that, resigns himself to a fatalism, and goes on.

Max comes to wisdom here, but something sexual is happening, too. On the literal level, perhaps the inevitable and natural experimenting. Whatever we are to make of it, the suggestion is there ("to slip into the spider's fingers . . . Max raised his sword . . . sheathed his point") and this prepares us for the Red Witch we run into around the other side of the pool.

At first she seems not to realize that Max is there, and he is allowed to watch her—naked, apparently, or nearly so, since he notices the color of her bosom. The new knowledge is still intellectual in nature, but this comes *through* an understanding which is to a considerable degree sexual ("Or one that combed so many obscene things/ From her black hair into her scarlet lap." . . . "Littlest and last Van Vrooman, do you come too?"/ She knew him . . . would know him better").

Max knows from what the witch says to him and because she appears to know him that he is not the first of his family to come here or to be *known* by the witch and realizes that his father has been here before him. Now an important part of his childhood is gone; his armor of "innocence" has a chink in it. Instinctively he strikes out to defend himself and his family with all he has, which is a threat—and one that is far from devoid of sexual implication, though in fairness let me say that Mr. Ransom has indicated that what sexuality there might be here was not deliberate.

"The scarlet hulk of hell with a fat bosom/ Pirouetting at the bottom of the forest" picks up the Dante theme again.

Max returns home chilled by the witch's laugh and her song (guilt?), and they linger with him, we imagine, when he plays on the lawn with his curls still unsmoothed.

MORNING

Jane awoke Ralph so gently on one morning
That first, before the true householder Learning
Came back to tenant in the haunted head,
He lay upon his back and let his stare
Penetrate dazedly into the blue air
That swam all round his bed,
And in the blessed silence nothing was said.

Then his eyes travelled through the window
And lit, enchantedly, on such a meadow
Of wings and light and clover,
He would propose to Jane then to go walking
Through the green waves, and to be singing not talking;
Such imps were pranking over
Him helpless lying in bed beneath a cover.

Suddenly he remembered about himself,
His manliness returned entire to Ralph;
The dutiful mills of the brain
Began to whir with their smooth-grinding wheels
And the sly visitors wriggled off like eels;
He rose and was himself again.
Simply another morning, and simply Jane.

Another treatment of the theme of dissociation. Ralph's body (spontaneity, first nature, unconsidered love) wakes up before his head does or, as the metaphor of the poem has it, the playful imps of particularity get to him ahead of "the true householder Learning." The air is a playful blue, uncontaminated by the cold tyranny of reason, and there is no need for language.

The bright image that opens the second stanza turns his eyes to butterflies, moving across a confusion of "wings and light and clover," until he wants to take his love and go with her where his eyes have gone "through the green waves." Still, we are told, and it is important, there would be no words. But then the householder returns, called now by another name: manliness. We are to assume that for Ralph there is no way to tell the difference between the two.

Whatever it was returned to Ralph, that anything returned "entire" "to tenant in" him is as ironic—sardonic—as the claim that it was manliness which did come. His problem is that there is nothing entire about him. He is compartmentalized, fragmented and dehumanized.

The dehumanization comes strongly in the line about the "mills" of the brain. They are "dutiful" mills. (As duty is a matter of honor, it is interesting to compare the poet's use of it here with his treatment of honor in "The Equilibrists."); it is confirmed by "whir" and "smooth-grinding wheels."

Then we see that what were imps before have become eels. We are seeing through Ralph's eyes; they are no longer pleasant things. They slither away, and now Ralph is numb to what is around him. The morning is still there. So is Jane. Ralph is not.

PHILOMELA

Procne, Philomela, and Itylus,
Your names are liquid, your improbable tale
Is recited in the classic numbers of the nightingale.
Ah, but our numbers are not felicitous,
It goes not liquidly for us.

Perched on a Roman ilex, and duly apostrophized,
The nightingale descanted unto Ovid;
She has even appeared to the Teutons, the swilled and gravid;
At Fontainebleau it may be the bird was gallicized;
Never was she baptized.

To England came Philomela with her pain,
Fleeing the hawk her husband; querulous ghost,
She wanders when he sits heavy on his roost,
Utters herself in the original again,
The untranslatable refrain.

Not to these shores she came; this other Thrace,
Environ barbarous to the royal Attic;
How could her delicate dirge run democratic,
Delivered in a cloudless boundless public place
To an inordinate race?

I pernoctated with the Oxford students once,
And in the quadrangles, in the cloisters, on the Cher,
Precociously knocked at antique doors ajar,
Fatuously touched the hems of the hierophants,
Sick of my dissonance.

71

I went out to Bagley Wood, I climbed the hill;
Even the moon had slanted off in a twinkling,
I heard the sepulchral owl and a few bells tinkling,
There was no more villainous day to unfulfil,
The diuturnity was still.

Out of the darkness where Philomela sat,
Her fairy numbers issued. What then ailed me?
My ears are called capacious but they failed me,
Her classics registered a little flat!
I rose, and venomously spat.

Philomela, Philomela, lover of song,
I am in despair if we may make us worthy,
A bantering breed sophistical and swarthy;
Unto more beautiful, persistently more young,
Thy fabulous provinces belong.

Ransom takes this most Greek of Greek myths—and by extension
the nightingale itself—to represent the poetry of the old world,
the classical sounds.[29]

"Numbers" in the first stanza refers, of course, to "people" as
well as to "poetry." The ilex is an oak, the tree which stands in
the center of a number of Ransom's poems, the Druid tree whose
roots, in a way we understand, are ours. One is tempted to say
that these are examples of the "irrelevancies," the wall-paper
texture adding excitement to the house, which is the structure
of the poem, except that such irrelevancies as these do a lot to
hold the structure of the poem together. The dichotomy is not
always a clear one.

"Descanted" echoes "apostrophized" in the sense of turning
aside, digressing from the main theme of a song for a variation,
as the Roman culture, represented here by Ovid, had much that
relationship to the Greek culture from which it borrowed so
heavily. The point here is that the nightingale was able to sing
in Rome at least an acceptable version of her song. And so for
even the rough and earthy Teuton and the Gaul.

Never, though, did she sing for the Christian; however much

of classical philosophy may have been adopted into Christian metaphysics, as Aristotle was converted by the intellectual sword of Aquinas, Christian art has never been comfortable for long without the leaf over David's private parts.

England, yes. But not America. Not even *secular* America, if there is one. As Thrace, however many colonies the Greeks could establish there, never absorbed the culture of the Greeks, so America has remained another world, barbarous, home of the "inordinate race." And inordinate here suggests both extraordinary and uncontrolled, without order. Formal balance is one of the distinguishing characteristics of Greek art and of her poetry. That kind of order is not a part of the new world.

Ransom introduces "pernoctated" to describe his all-night talks with other students at Oxford because this was the word he learned to use there when he was doing it. The students were in the habit of carrying on all night, and in order to discourage the practice the dormitory proctor checked the beds of the students each morning. If the bed showed that it had not been slept in the student was called up and charged with pernoctating.

There is a richness of suggestion in the use of "hierophants." The specific and original reference is to the high priest of the Eleusinian mysteries in Greek religion. The worship of Dionysus, one of the gods who figured importantly in these mysteries, is said to have been imported from Thrace. If this hardly brings us full circle, we have the satisfying sense of a completed circle tangent to our own.

"Unfulfil," one of the negative inventions Ransom likes to use, is not put here simply for freshness of expression, as such words rarely are in his poems. It is not the same as the verb "to empty," which is an undoing of what has been done; nor is it the same as "not fulfil," which implies no more than passivity, as if we were leaving things no worse, if no better, than we found them. "Unfulfil" is an active verb. It is an undoing of what has not been done.

When the speaker in the poems climbs a hill to hear the song of the nightingale, we see, ironically, the form of the Greek tragedy: peripety and recognition come quickly. He realizes not only that he cannot bring the bird to America but that now, having listened carefully to her song, he finds it a little flat! Still he assumes for his own land the burden of failure, but he resigns himself to that and leaves the nightingale to her "fabulous provinces," implying perhaps in the words that America, a "bantering breed sophistical and swarthy," is somehow the center of a world of its own and that there is something of the provincial even about the old world, at least by some atlas.

If there is despair in this, there is a feeling also of resolution that it will not be necesary any longer to be sickened by the dissonance. The speaker has climbed from the world as he had thought it ought to be to the world as it is, from fancy to a matter of fact. In this especially "Philomela" is very much a poem of Ransom's.

PERSISTENT EXPLORER

The noise of water teased his literal ear
Which heard the distant drumming, and so scored:
"Water is falling—it fell—therefore it roared.
Yet something else is there: is it cheer or fear?"

He strode much faster, till on the dizzy brink
His eye confirmed with vision what he'd heard:
"A simple physical water." Again he demurred:
"More than a roaring flashing water, I think."

But listen as he might, look fast or slow,
It was common water, millions of tons of it
Gouging its gorge deeper, and every bit
Was water, the insipid chemical H_2O.

Its thunder smote him somewhat as the loud
Words of the god that rang around a man
Walking by the Mediterranean.
Its cloud of froth was whiter than the cloud

That clothed the goddess sliding down the air
Unto a mountain shepherd, white as she
That issued from the smoke refulgently.
The cloud was, but the goddess was not there.

Deafening was the sound, but never a voice
That talked with him; spacious the spectacle
But it spelled nothing; there was not any spell
Whether to bid him cower or rejoice.

What would he have it spell? He scarcely knew;
Only that water and nothing but water filled
His eyes and ears; only water that spilled;
And if the smoke and rattle of water drew

From the deep thickets of his mind the train,
The fierce fauns and the timid tenants there
That burst their bonds and rushed upon the air,
Why, he must turn and beat them down again.

So be it. And no unreasonable outcry
The pilgrim made; only a rueful grin
Spread over his lips until he drew them in;
He would not sit upon a rock and die.

Many are the ways of dying; witness, if he
Commit himself to the water, and descend
Wrapped in the water, turn water at the end,
Part of a water rolling to the sea.

But there were many ways of living, too,
And let his enemies gibe, but let them say
That he would throw this continent away
And seek another country—as he would do.

Here is the literal man, the dissociated creature—Ralph, of
"Morning," perhaps—who has decided to get up after all and see
what it is there outside the window. He feels pretty sure at first

that whatever is going on his intellect can deal with: "Water is falling—it fell—therefore it roared." We can almost hear him saying, as he strokes his chin thoughtfully, "Post hoc, ergo propter hoc." This is the spiritual cousin to the friar of "Necrological," with reasoned answers to everything.

There is a brief struggle as the man, sensing that something here is not coming through to him, doubts his eyes for a moment. But fact wins over truth, and the substance is analyzed and located on the periodic table. There is no mystery. It is the insipid chemical H_2O. To the imagination, to the mind that creates and is created by myth, it is more than this. It is something the Explorer catches only a slight intimation of. For him there is no revelation, there is no goddess in the cloud, no voice in the sound, no spell in the spectacle. As the pun has it, there is no meaning, no message.

Our suspicion that we have met this man before is heightened when we discover that there are "timid tenants" hiding in him, that he beats them back if they get out into the air. Surely this is Ralph.

"Unreasonable" as it is used here means "unreasoned, uncontrolled by the head; unintellectualized." The young man keeps the myth-makers in check.

He could find his life, to go back some, by losing it; he could drown to salvation. One thinks of Prufrock and the chambers of the sea. But there is a simpler way—it appears—to avoid the confusion, the frustration of this predicament. He can get himself to where there are no such waterfalls, no such clouds. He can live in the flatland. And that is what he will do.

OF MARGARET

Frost, and a leaf has quit the tulip tree
Wafting on brightest airs with twist and turn;
The wafer body is Margaret's first-born.
A day of dark shall be her Calvary.

Then shall the leaves be stained with weathering,
And the green sward of a sudden be defiled
With surfeit, till one soft wind of grace unchild
Her of the sons of all her mothering.

No mother sorrow is but follows birth,
And beyond that, conception; hers was large,
And so immoderate love must be a scourge
Needing the whole ecstasy of substant earth.

But no evil shall spot this, Margaret's page.
The generations born of her loving mood
Were modes of yellow greenery, not of blood,
And the faithful issue was blossom and foliage.

Virgin, whose bravest image in the grass
I keep against this tide of wayfaring,
O hear the maiden pageant ever sing
Of that far away time of gentleness.

Several of the people who live in Ransom's poems have a great attachment for the things of nature. It is common to feel a nostalgia when autumn settles over everything, but usually the feeling is vague and fleeting; certainly grief is too strong a word to describe it. But Margaret is grieved. Just as Conrad, who must be her kinsman, is grieved. And as Miriam, who is another cousin, is grieved.

Such grief as Margaret's and her name bring to mind Hopkins' poem "Spring and Fall: to a Young Child," in which an earlier Margaret is filled with sadness at the falling of the leaves. But it is different in Hopkins' poem. His girl mourns not for the leaves, but for herself; it is not the passing of the season, but the mortality it symbolizes that disturbs her. Hopkins tells her so:

> It is the blight man was born for,
> It is Margaret you mourn for.

77

Not so with Ransom's people. Margaret, Conrad—even poor Miriam, hard as her flowers try to be symbols—are mourning for the things themselves: the very leaves. In fact, "Conrad Sits in Twilight" was revised eventually to "Master's in the Garden Again" partly to make it clear that the poem was *not* about a man mourning his own years. The poem is not a metaphor.

Margaret is so close to the plants that she seems to herself a tree and the leaves her children. The poet is quick to tell us, however, that it is all "as if," that Margaret has no children of her own blood. She is a virgin. So, as we remember, was Miriam a virgin. It is rarely easy to decide exactly where Ransom's own feelings lie. We can bring ourselves to think that Miriam was foolish and went too far and to think that Ransom thought so. With Margaret it is different. There is an elevation here, at the end almost an invocation, a song of praise for the grace and beauty of Margaret's world.

The blind land is filling now with her dead children, and the wind will "unchild/ Her" of the last of them. But this is no Miriam Tazewell, finally, and it was no unseasonal violence that took her family. We can see her pregnant again during the long winter, her virgin belly as round as the substant—the standing-under, the understanding—earth.

THE VANITY OF THE BRIGHT BOYS

There is, as Ransom has said in a recent letter, "something of a scholarly stunt, a *tour de force,* where a critic pores over the old worksheets of a writer." What I am about here is not a poring over, but rather I want to show—without any comment, except for a brief discussion after the final version of the poem—something of the changes that may occur in a poem on its way to being finished in the poet's mind and the changes that have taken place in the mind of the poet as these are reflected in the poem's development over a number of years.

If the explication of the version of a poem which a writer comes to as the finished poem can serve in opening the way into his poems, then the movement through another dimension, the developing versions, ought to deepen the reader's insight both into the poem and the poet. To that end, here are nine versions of "The Vanity of the Bright Boys," running from its appearance as "Tom, Tom, the Piper's Son" in *Chills and Fevers* in 1924 through revisions in typescript made after the appearance of the 1963 *Selected Poems,* and ending with the version printed in the 1969 edition.

The versions are numbered in sequence. Except for the first and last, each is printed twice, so as to appear on the page facing the one from which it was revised.

1 TOM, TOM, THE PIPER'S SON

Grim in my little black coat as the sleazy beetle,
And gone of hue,
Lonely, a man reputed for softening little,
Loving few—

Mournfully going where men assemble, unfriended, pushing
With laborious wares,
And glaring with little grey eyes at whom I am brushing,
Who would with theirs—

Full of my thoughts as I trudge here and trundle yonder,
Eyes on the ground,
Tricked by white birds or tall women into no wonder,
And no sound—

Yet privy to great dreams, and secret in vainglory,
And hot and proud,
And poor and bewildered, and longing to hear my own story
Rehearsed aloud—

How I have passed, involved in these chances and choices,
By certain trees
Whose tiny attent auricles receive the true voices
Of the wordless breeze—

And against me the councils of spirits were not then darkened
Who thereby house,
As I set my boots to the path beneath them, and hearkened
To the talking boughs—

How one said, "This ambulant worm, he is strangely other
Than they suppose"—
But one, "He was sired by his father and dammed by his mother,
And acknowledges those"

2 THE VANITY OF THE MALE

Grim in my little black coat as the sleazy beetle,
And gone of hue,
Lonely, a man reputed for softening little,
Loving few—

Entering into the houses, unfriended, pushing
With laborious wares,
And glaring with little grey eyes at whom I was brushing,
Who would with theirs—

Or full of thoughts as I trudged here and yonder,
Eyes on the ground,
Till loud birds or bright women made in my eyes no wonder,
In my ears no sound—

How huge I towered in that dreamt-of vainglory,
And hot and proud,
And poor and bewildered, and longing to hear my story
Rehearsed aloud—

And once or twice I passed, in the luck of my choices,
By certain trees
Whose turning auricles at last received true voices
Of the favoring breeze—

* And against me the councils of spirits were not then darkened
Who thereby house,
As I set my boots to the path beneath them, and hearkened
To the talking boughs—

How one said, "This ambulant worm, he is strangely other
Than they suppose"—
But one, "He was sired by his father and dammed by his mother,
And acknowledges those"—

* Only the first five stanzas of this version have been saved. The last five
stanzas are repeated from the first version for continuity.

81

And then: "Nay, nay—this man is a changeling, and knows not—
This was a Prince
From a far great kingdom—and should return, but goes not—
Long years since"—

But like a King I was subject to a King's condition,
And I marched on,
Not testing at eavesdrop the glory of my suspicion,
And the talkers were gone—

And duly appeared I on the very clock-throb appointed
In the litten room,
Nor was hailed with that love that leaps to the Heir Anointed:
"Hush, hush, he is come!"

And then: "Nay, nay—this man is a changeling, and knows not—
This was a Prince
From a far great kingdom—and should return, but goes not—
Long years since"—

But like a king I was subject to a king's condition,
And I marched on,
Not testing at eavesdrop the glory of my suspicion,
And the talkers were gone—

And duly appeared I on the very clock-throb appointed
In the litten room,
Nor was hailed with that love that leaps to the Heir Anointed:
"Hush, hush, he is come!"

Grim in my little black suit as the sleazy beetle,
And gone of hue,
Lonely, a man reputed for softening little,
Loving few—

Entering into the houses, unfriended, pushing
With laborious wares,
And glaring with little grey eyes at whom I was brushing,
Who would with theirs—

Or full of thoughts as I trudged here and yonder,
Eyes on the ground,
Till loud birds or bright women made in my eyes no wonder,
in my ears no sound—

How huge I towered in that dreamt-of vainglory,
And hot and proud,
And poor and bewildered, and longing to hear my story
Rehearsed aloud—

And once or twice I passed, in the luck of my choices,
By certain trees
Whose turning auricles at last received true voices
Of the favoring breeze—

And against me the councils of spirits were not then darkened
Who thereby house,
As I set my boots to the path beneath them, and hearkened
To the talking boughs—

How one said, "This ambulant worm, he is strangely other
Than they suppose"—
But one, "He was sired by his father and dammed by his mother,
And acknowledges those"—

84

3 THE VANITY OF THE BRIGHT YOUNG MEN

You think in my tight black coat I'm like a beetle.
I never mind my looks,
I'm removed, a boy reported not liking people,
My familiars mostly are books.

I go alone to assembly, but I'd go pushing
Even to say my prayers,
Glaring with cold grey eyes at whom I am brushing,
Who would if they could with theirs.

But afternoons I walk in the primal creation,
In a spell, in a possible glory,
Counting on Nature to give me an intimation
Of my unlikely story.

One time I went, by the luck of my chances and choices,
Past certain Druid trees
Whose leaves were ears and tongues translating the voices
Hid in the muffling breeze.

Against me the councils of spirits were not then darkened
Though out of my vision or reach,
As I set my boots to the path beneath and hearkened
Unto phrases of English speech.

One said, "This worm of the dust—he is strangely other
Than he and they suppose"—
But one, "Yet sired by his father and dammed by his mother?
Has he not acknowledged those?"

Again, "But wait—this man is a changeling but knows not—
I tell you this is a Prince"—
"From a far great kingdom and should return but goes not?"
Fifteen long winters since"—

And then: "Nay, nay—this man is a changeling, and knows not—
This was a Prince
From a far great kingdom—and should return, but goes not—
Long years since"—

But like a King I was subject to a King's condition,
And I marched on,
Not testing at eavesdrop the glory of my suspicion,
And the talkers were gone—

And duly appeared I on the very clock-throb appointed
In the litten room,
Nor was hailed with that love that leaps to the Heir Anointed:
"Hush, hush, he is come!"

But like a king I was bound to a king's condition.
I steadied and marched right on,
Not testing by eavesdrop the wonder of my suspicion,
And quick that talk was gone.

And prompt I showed, as the tower's last throb appointed,
In the loud and litten room
Nor was hailed by that love that leaps to the Heir Anointed:
"Hush, O hush, he is come."

3 THE VANITY OF THE BRIGHT YOUNG MEN

You think in my tight black coat I'm like a beetle.
I never mind my looks,
I'm removed, a boy reported not liking people,
My familiars mostly are books.

I go alone to assembly, but I'd go pushing
Even to say my prayers
Glaring with cold grey eyes at whom I am brushing,
Who would if they could with theirs.

But afternoons I walk in the primal creation,
In a spell, in a possible glory,
Counting on Nature to give me on intimation
Of my unlikely story.

One time I went, by the luck of my chances and choices,
Past certain Druid trees
Whose leaves were ears and tongues translating the voices
Hid in the muffling breeze.

Against me the councils of spirits were not then darkened
Though out of my vision or reach,
As I set my boots to the path beneath and hearkened
Unto phrases of English speech.

One said, "This worm of the dust—he is strangely other
Than he and they suppose"—
But one, "Yet sired by his father and dammed by his mother?
Has he not acknowledged those?"

Again, "But wait—this man is a changeling but knows not—
I tell you this is a Prince"—
"From a far great kingdom and should return but goes not?"
Fifteen long winters since"—

4 THE VANITY OF THE BRIGHT YOUNG MEN

Absurd in my tight black coat like a sleazy beetle
I wasn't minding my looks,
I was looking at me, the boy bereaved of a title
Minding his dreams and books.

To assembly I walked alone, but forever pushing
Even to say my prayers,
Glaring with coldest eyes at whom I was brushing
Who would, if they could, with theirs.

In late afternoons I walked in our furthermost forest
And wasted for my miracle,
Should a blackbird sit on my arm reciting the merest
Syllables of my oracle.

Happening once by luck of my chances and choices
On the dark Druid trees,
Scholars and chosen, translators of strange voices
Stitched in the wind's wheeze,

I shortened stride at a shrubbery, where two together
Might parley, and question rise;

One saying, "This boy who tugs at tether may be other
Than he and they suppose."
But one, "Yet sired and dammed by a father and mother
And surely acknowledges those?"

"The sweet babe royal, if he was changed not knowing
Yet still assumes the Prince"—
"A King to be? And his sword and crest not showing?"
"Fourteen long winters since!"

But like a king I was bound to a king's condition.
I steadied and marched right on,
Not testing by eavesdrop the wonder of my suspicion,
And quick that talk was gone.

And prompt I showed, as the tower's last throb appointed,
In the loud and litten room
Nor was hailed by that love that leaps to the Heir Anointed:
"Hush, O hush, he is come."

Then almost I was absolved of a maimed ambition
And tired royal blood;

And malingering Prince from whose singular vegetation
I sprang to my regular stride,
Stopping eavesdropping for a wavering name and nation
From wranglers wide as the wood,

Homecoming just as the tower's last throb expired
In the loud unlistening room,
In babble and rabble. O if they'd stared and adored
Crying "Look, hush, he has come!"

Absurd in my tight black coat like a sleazy beetle
I wasn't minding my looks,
I was looking at me, the boy bereaved of a title
Minding his dreams and books.

To assembly I walked alone, but forever pushing
Even to say my prayers,
Glaring with coldest eyes at whom I was brushing
Who would, if they could, with theirs.

In late afternoons I walked in our furthermost forest
And wasted for my miracle,
Should a blackbird sit on my arm reciting the merest
Syllables of my oracle.

Happening once by luck of my chances and choices
On the dark Druid trees,
Scholars and chosen, translators of strange voices
Stitched in the wind's wheeze,

I shortened stride at a shrubbery, where two together
Might parley, and question rise;

One saying, "This boy who tugs at tether may be other
Than he and they suppose."
But one, "Yet sired and dammed by a father and mother
And surely acknowledges those?"

"The sweet babe royal, if he was changed not knowing
Yet still assumes the Prince"—
"A King to be? And his sword and crest not showing?"
"Fourteen long winters since!"

Then almost I was absolved of a maimed ambition
And tired royal blood;

5 THE VANITY OF THE BRIGHT YOUNG MEN

Absurd in my tight black coat like a sleazy beetle
I wasn't minding my looks,
I was looking at me, the boy bereaved of a title
Minding his dreams and books.

To assembly I walked alone, but forever pushing
Even to say my prayers,
Glaring with coldest eyes at whom I was brushing
Who would, if they could, with theirs.

In late afternoons I walked in a green fable
And wasted for my miracle,
Should a yellow beak intone from a throat of sable
The syllables of an oracle.

Happening once by luck of my chances and choices
Beside those Druid trees,
Rulers but scholars, translators of strange voices
Stitched in the wind's wheeze,

I shortened stride at a shrubbery, where two together
Parleyed, and question rose;

One saying, "This boy who tugs at tether may be other
Than he and they suppose"—
But one, "Yet sired and dammed by a father and mother
And surely acknowledges those?"

"The sweet babe royal, if he was changed not knowing
Yet still assumes the Prince"—
"A King to be? with his sword and crest not showing?"
"Fourteen long winters since"—

Then almost I was absolved of a maimed ambition
And tired royal blood;

And malingering Prince from whose singular vegetation
I sprang to my regular stride,
Stopping eavesdropping for a wavering name and nation
From wranglers wide as the wood,

Homecoming just as the tower's last throb expired
In the loud unlistening room,
In babble and rabble. O if they'd stared and adored
Crying "Look, hush, he has come!"

And malingering Prince from whose singular vegetation
I sprang to my regular stride,
Stopping eavesdropping for a wavering name and nation
From wranglers wide as the wood,

Homecoming just as the tower's last throb expired
In the loud unlistening room,
In babble and rabble. O if they'd stared and adored
Crying "Look, hush, he has come!"

Absurd in my tight black coat like a sleazy beetle
I wasn't minding my looks,
I was looking at me, the boy bereaved of a title
Minding his dreams and books.

To assembly I walked alone, but forever pushing
Even to say my prayers,
Glaring with coldest eyes at whom I was brushing
Who would, if they could, with theirs.

In late afternoons I walked in a green fable
And wasted for my miracle,
Should a yellow beak intòne from a throat of sable
The syllables of an oracle.

Happening once by luck of my chances and choices
Beside those Druid trees,
Rulers but scholars, translators of strange voices
Stitched in the wind's wheeze,

I shortened stride at a shrubbery, where two together
Parleyed, and question rose;

One saying, "This boy who tugs at tether may be other
Than he and they suppose"—
But one, "Yet sired and dammed by a father and mother
And surely acknowledges those?"

"The sweet babe royal, if he was changed not knowing
Yet still assumes the Prince"—
"A King to be? with his sword and crest not showing?"
"Fourteen long winters since"—

Then almost I was absolved of a maimed ambition
And tired royal blood;

Absurd in my tight black coat like a sleazy beetle
I wasn't minding my looks,
I was looking at me, the boy bereaved of a title
Minding his dreams and books.

To assembly I walked alone, but forever pushing
Even to say my prayers,
Glaring with coldest eyes at whom I was brushing
Who would, if they could, with theirs.

In late afternoons I walked in a green fable
And wasted for my miracle,
Should a yellow beak intone from a throat of sable
One syllable of an oracle.

Happening once by luck of my chances and choices
On the holy Druid trees,
Rulers whose leaves translate the truculent voices
Stitched on the wind's wheeze,

I shortened stride at a shrubbery, where two together
Parleyed, and question rose;

One saying, "This boy who tugs at tether may be other
Than he and they suppose"—
But one, "Yet sired and dammed by a father and mother
And surely acknowledges those?"

"That sweet babe royal, if he was changed not knowing
Yet still he plays the Prince"—
"A King to be? with his sword and crest not showing?"
"Fourteen long winters since"—

Then almost I was absolved of a maimed ambition
And tired royal blood;

And malingering Prince from whose singular vegetation
I sprang to my regular stride,
Stopping eavesdropping for a wavering name and nation
From wranglers wide as the wood,

Homecoming just as the tower's last throb expired
In the loud unlistening room,
In babble and rabble. O if they'd stared and adored
Crying "Look, hush, he has come!"

And malingering Prince from whose singular vegetation
I sprang to my regular stride,
Stopping eavesdropping for a wavering name and nation
From wranglers wide as the wood,

To see if I throve where a tower's last throb expired
And was dumb in the unlistening room
Where a rabble babbled. O if they'd stared and adored
Crying "Look, hush, he has come!"

Absurd in my tight black coat like a sleazy beetle
I wasn't minding my looks,
I was looking at me, the boy bereaved of a title
Minding his dreams and books.

To assembly I walked alone, but forever pushing
Even to say my prayers,
Glaring with coldest eyes at whom I was brushing
Who would, if they could, with theirs.

In late afternoons I walked in a green fable
And wasted for my miracle,
Should a yellow beak intone from a throat of sable
One syllable of an oracle.

Happening once by luck of my chances and choices
On the holy Druid trees,
Rulers whose leaves translate the truculent voices
Stitched on the wind's wheeze,

I shortened stride at a shrubbery, where two together
Parleyed, and question rose;

One saying, "This boy who tugs at tether may be other
Than he and they suppose"—
But one, "Yet sired and dammed by a father and mother
And surely acknowledges those?"

"That sweet babe royal, if he was changed not knowing
Yet still he plays the Prince"—
"A King to be? with his sword and crest not showing?"
"Fourteen long winters since"—

Then almost I was absolved of a maimed ambition
And tired royal blood;

Absurd in my tight black coat like a sleazy beetle
I wasn't minding my looks,
I was looking at me, the boy bereaved of a title
Minding his dreams and books.

To assembly I walked alone, but forever pushing
Even to say my prayers,
Glaring with coldest eyes at whom I was brushing
Who would, if they could, with theirs.

In late afternoons I strode in a green fable
And wasted for my miracle,
Should a yellow beak intone from a throat of sable
One syllable of an oracle.

Happening once by luck of my chances and choices
On the holy Druid trees
Rulers whose leaves translate the truculent voices
Stitched in the wind's wheeze,

I shortened stride at a shrubbery, where two together
Parleyed, and question rose;

One saying, "This boy who tugs at tether may be other
Than he and they suppose"—
But one, "Yet sired and dammed by a father and mother
And surely acknowledges those?"

"That sweet babe royal, if he was changed not knowing
But still he plays the Prince"—
"A King to be? With his sword and crest not showing"—
"Fourteen long winters since"—

Then almost I was absolved of my brainwashed ambition
And tired royal blood;

And malingering Prince from whose singular vegetation
I sprang to my regular stride,
Stopping eavesdropping for a wavering name and nation
From wranglers wide as the wood,

To see if I throve where a tower's last throb expired
And was dumb in the unlistening room
Where a rabble babbled. O if they'd stared and adored
Crying "Look, hush, he has come!"

And malingering Prince, from whose vegetary operation
I sprang to my ravening stride
(Stopping eavesdropping for a wavering name and nation
From wranglers ever wide)

To see if I throve where a tower's deep throb expired
And was dumb in the unlistening room
Where a rabble babbled. O if they'd stared and adored
Crying "Look, hush, he has come!"

Nobody cried. Some touched him and welcomed him home
As blest because he had come.

Absurd in my tight black coat like a sleazy beetle
I wasn't minding my looks,
I was looking at me, the boy bereaved of a title
Minding his dreams and books.

To assembly I walked alone, but forever pushing
Even to say my prayers,
Glaring with coldest eyes at whom I was brushing
Who would, if they could, with theirs.

In late afternoons I strode in a green fable
And wasted for my miracle,
Should a yellow beak intone from a throat of sable
One syllable of an oracle.

Happening once by luck of my chances and choices
On the holy Druid trees
Rulers whose leaves translate the truculent voices
Stitched in the wind's wheeze,

I shortened stride at a shrubbery, where two together
Parleyed, and question rose;

One saying, "This boy who tugs at tether may be other
Than he and they suppose"—
But one, "Yet sired and dammed by a father and mother
And surely acknowledges those?"

"That sweet babe royal, if he was changed not knowing
But still he plays the Prince"—
"A King to be? With his sword and crest not showing"—
"Fourteen long winters since"—

Then almost I was absolved of my brainwashed ambition
And tired royal blood;

104

Absurd in my tight black coat like a sleazy beetle
I wasn't minding my looks,
I was looking at me, the boy bereaved of a title
Minding his dreams and books.

To assembly I walked alone, but forever pushing
Even to say my prayers,
Glaring with coldest eyes at whom I was brushing
Who would, if they could, with theirs.

In late afternoons I walked in a green fable
And wasted for my miracle,
Should a yellow beak intone from a throat of sable
One syllable of an Oracle.

Happening once by luck of my chances and choices
On the holy Druid trees,
Rulers whose leaves translate the truculent voices
Stitched in the wind's wheeze,

I shortened stride at a shrubbery, where two together
Parleyed, and question rose;

One saying, "This boy who tugs at tether may be other
Than he and they suppose"—
But one, "Yet sired and dammed by a father and mother
And surely acknowledges those?"

"That sweet babe royal, if he was changed not knowing
But still he plays the Prince"—
"A King to be? with his sword and crest not showing"
"Fourteen long winters since"—

Then almost I was absolved of my brainwashed ambition
And tired royal blood;

And malingering Prince, from whose vegetary operation
I sprang to my ravening stride
(Stopping eavesdropping for a wavering name and nation
From wranglers ever wide)

To see if I throve where a tower's deep throb expired
And was dumb in the unlistening room
Where a rabble babbled. O if they'd stared and adored
Crying "Look, hush, he has come!"

Nobody cried. Some touched him and welcomed him home
As blest because he had come.

And malingering Prince, from whose vegetary operation
I sprang to my ravening stride,
Stopping eavesdropping for a wavering name and nation
From wranglers always wide,

To see how I throve where the tower's deep throb expired
And was dumb in the unlistening room
Where a rabble babbled. O, if they'd stared and adored
Crying "Look, hush, he has come!"

Nobody cried. Some touched the bright boy returning
As blest for having him home,
Who smiled and sat; if he took no joy of journeying
Let him make his kingdom come.

Absurd in my tight black coat like a sleazy beetle
I wasn't minding my looks,
I was looking at me, the boy bereaved of a title
Minding his dreams and books.

To assembly I walked alone, but forever pushing
Even to say my prayers,
Glaring with coldest eyes at whom I was brushing
Who would, if they could, with theirs.

In late afternoons I walked in a green fable
And wasted for my miracle,
Should a yellow beak intone from a throat of sable
One syllable of an Oracle.

Happening once by luck of my chances and choices
On the holy Druid trees,
Rulers whose leaves translate the truculent voices
Stitched in the wind's wheeze,

I shortened stride at a shrubbery, where two together
Parleyed, and question rose;

One saying, "This boy who tugs at tether may be other
Than he and they suppose"—
But one, "Yet sired and dammed by a father and mother
And surely acknowledges those?"

"That sweet babe royal, if he was changed not knowing
But still he plays the Prince"—
"A King to be? with his sword and crest not showing"
"Fourteen long winters since"—

Then almost I was absolved of my brainwashed ambition
And tired royal blood;

108

Absurd in his tight black coat like a sleazy beetle
He wasn't minding his looks,
He looked inside, at the boy bereaved of his title
Minding his dreams and books.

To assembly he walked alone, but forever pushing
Even to say his prayers,
Glaring with coldest eyes at whom he was brushing
Who could, if they would, with theirs.

In late afternoons he walked in a green fable
And wasted for his miracle,
Should a yellow beak intone from a throat of sable
One syllable of his Oracle.

Even walking he dreamed; and partial in his choices
He called on the Druid trees,
Dark gods whose leaves translated the judgment voices
Stitched in the wind's wheeze;

He shortened stride at a shrubbery where two together
Parleyed, and question rose:

One saying, "The boy who tugs at tether may be other
Than he and they suppose."
But one, "Yet sired and dammed by a father and mother
And you have record of those?"

"That sweet babe royal, if he was changed unknowing
Though still he plays the Prince—"
"A King to be? With his sword and crest not showing?"
"Fifteen long winters since—"

He awoke, ashamed, absolved of brain-washed ambition
And tired royal blood;

And malingering Prince, from whose vegetary operation
I sprang to my ravening stride,
Stopping eavesdropping for a wavering name and nation
From wranglers always wide,

To see how I throve where the tower's deep throb expired
And was dumb in the unlistening room
Where a rabble babbled. O, if they'd stared and adored
Crying "Look, hush, he has come!"

Nobody cried. Some touched the bright boy returning
As blest for having him home,
Who smiled and sat; if he took no joy of journeying
Let him make his kingdom come.

Of malingering Prince, from whose vegetary operation
He sprang to his ravening stride—

Stopping eavesdropping for wavering name and nation
From wrangling ghosts and wide—

To see if he throve where the tower's last throb expired
And was dumb in the unlistening room
And the babble of boys. O if they'd stared and adored
Crying "Look, hush, he has come!"

No; but they waved a welcome to bright boy returning
As blest for having him there,
Who laughed and sat; with only an instant's mourning
For castles in the air.

The evening's orator rose to his height of speaking
And wantoned with Heaven and Doom;
The boy indifferent; all that long Night of Waking
Addressing his blessings at home.

L'ENVOI

Dawn, you've purpled a politic Prince,
He's done no running and peeking since,
Thrones are trash, and Kings are dumb,
Say, would he rather his kingdom come?

111

There has been a consistent and subtle change in the poet's attitude toward the bright young men, the bright boys, a growing sympathy shown in the substitution of words and phrases which draw forth compassion and create a feeling of pathos. The boy in the poem is not so pretentious as he was, not quite so cocky. We almost wish he might find his parents royal. But the most important change is in the ending. Ransom has not been satisfied just to leave the boy lost in his delusions; he gives us some hope that he might make the best of the affection he finds for himself as an ordinary person and might even be happy with it.

This is the direction of the change, and the motive behind the change, in "Prelude to an Evening," as Ransom has explained in his long critical comment on it in his *Selected Poems* (1963). In both cases, he returned to the poems not to make technical or stylistic improvements, but to do better by the people there. In "Prelude to an Evening" the change to this better condition was dictated by overriding philosophical considerations. Whether the *human* concern behind the change in the closing of "The Vanity of the Bright Boys" is consistent with the *aesthetic* concern, or ought to override it, is something else. I suspect that the poem may suffer for the sake of the boy; I suspect also that Ransom may quite gladly have made that choice.

OLD MANSION
(*After Henry James*)

As an intruder I trudged with careful innocence
To mask in decency a meddlesome stare,
Passing the old house often on its eminence,
Exhaling my foreign weed on its weighted air.

Here age seemed newly imagined for the historian
After his monstrous château on the Loire,
A beauty not for depicting by old vulgarian
Reiterations that gentle readers abhor.

112

It was a Southern manor. One hardly imagines
Towers, arcades, or forbidding fortress walls;
But sufficient state though its peacocks now were pigeons;
Where no courts kept, but grave rites and funerals.

Indeed, not distant, possibly not external
To the property, were tombstones, where the catafalque
Had carried their dead; and projected a note too charnel
But for the honeysuckle on its intricate stalk.

Stability was the character of its rectangle
Whose line was seen in part and guessed in part
Through trees. Decay was the tone of old brick and shingle.
Green shutters dragging frightened the watchful heart

To assert: Your mansion, long and richly inhabited,
Its porches and bowers suiting the children of men,
Will not forever be thus, O man, exhibited,
And one had best hurry to enter it if one can.

And at last, with my happier angel's own temerity,
Did I clang their brazen knocker against the door,
To beg their dole of a look, in simple charity,
Or crumbs of wisdom dropping from their great store.

But it came to nothing—and may so gross denial
Which has been deplored with a beating of the breast
Never shorten the tired historian, loyal
To acknowledge defeat and discover a new quest.

The old mistress was ill, and sent my dismissal
By one even more wrappered and lean and dark
Than that warped concierge and imperturbable vassal
Who had bid me begone from her master's Gothic park.

Emphatically, the old house crumbled; the ruins
Would litter, as already the leaves, this petted sward;
And no annalist went in to the lords or the peons;
The antiquary would finger the bits of shard.

113

But on retreating I saw myself in the token,
How loving from my dying weed the feather curled
On the lanquid air; and I went with courage shaken
To dip, alas, into some unseemlier world.

Of Ransom's poems, only "Blackberry Winter," "Man without Sense of Direction," "Antique Harvesters" and this one are specifically, identifiably Southern. Ransom doesn't call himself a "Southern poet," but the Southerner and the poet continually confront one another. In these poems the confrontation is direct.

At the time of the writing of "Old Mansion" he was taken with the writings of Henry James and the idea of exile. He had himself just returned from Europe ("Exhaling my foreign weed") and wanted to know if it might after all be possible to come home again. He found that the home was changing even more rapidly perhaps than the traveller was.

After the publication of the 1963 edition, Ransom added a new third stanza, and then decided to drop it again before the 1969 edition went to press. The poem will stand as the poet leaves it, but it is interesting to see what the temporary third stanza added, which was something not said clearly otherwise: that the passing of the Old Mansion and all it stands for is as if it were a part of the natural order of things, a part of the natural turning of the world, as if the house itself were turning like a tree in the fall.

Surrounded by a sense of death and decline, the speaker gives himself over to his brighter spirit, summons his courage and asks to be let in, if by nothing more than charity, if for nothing more than a crumb of the wisdom which the old house must hold. He is refused and descants to hope that the historian will not be so easily put off.

"The old mistress was ill," he says, and we are reminded of the opening line of "Blackberry Winter": "If there be a power of sweetness, let it lie." In the 1963 edition the echo was even stronger: "If the lady hath any loveliness, let it die."

The Negro who comes to the door is significantly stronger than the mistress, has outlasted her to inherit by default the crumbling society, and has become its curator and its protector. The

Negro does not welcome the exile, who was no more successful in getting past the "warped concierge" of Europe. He has become a provincial without a province.

"Emphatically," which opens the next stanza, may be Ransom's most subtle and esoteric double use of a word. He has pointed out that the allied Greek root ἐμφατικός suggests "significant," so that the sense of meaning, of reason behind what is happening, is underscored. The house did not just happen to crumble.

Finally the exile knows that he will not return to what is no longer and goes away, not to enter into another culture, but to "dip"—it is an important word—"into some unseemlier world."

Here, maintaining the marvelous slant rhymes on the first and third lines which account for much of the muted tone of this poem, is the third stanza that Ransom introduced between the 1963 and 1969 editions:

> Each time of seeing I absorbed some other feature
> Of a house whose annals in no wise could be brief
> Nor ignoble; for it expired as sweetly as Nature,
> With her tinge as of oxidation on autumn leaf.

MAN WITHOUT SENSE OF DIRECTION

> Tell this to ladies: how a hero man
> Assail a thick and scandalous giant
> Who casts true shadow in the sun,
> And die, but play no truant.
>
> This is more horrible: that the darling egg
> Of the chosen people hatch a creature
> Of noblest mind and powerful leg
> Who cannot fathom nor perform his nature.
>
> The larks' tongues are never stilled
> Where the pale spread straw of sunlight lies;
> Then what invidious gods have willed
> Him to be seized so otherwise?

115

Birds of the field and beasts of the stable
Are swollen with rapture and make uncouth
Demonstration of joy, which is a babble
Offending the ear of the fervorless youth.

Love—is it the cause? the proud shamed spirit?
Love has slain some whom it possessed,
But his was requited beyond his merit
And won him in bridal the loveliest.

Yet scarcely he issues from the warm chamber,
Flushed with her passion, when cold as dead
Once more he walks where waves past number
Of sorrow buffet his curse-hung head.

Whether by street, or in field full of honey,
Attended by clouds of the creatures of air
Or shouldering the city's companioning many,
His doom is on him; and how can he care

For the shapes that would fiddle upon his senses,
Wings and faces and mists that move,
Words, sunlight, the blue air which rinses
The pure pale head which he must love?

And he writhes like an antique man of bronze
That is beaten by furies visible,
Yet he is punished not knowing his sins
And for his innocence walks in hell.

He flails his arms, he moves his lips:
"Rage have I none, cause, time, nor country—
Yet I have traveled land and ships
And knelt my seasons in the chantry."

So he stands muttering; and rushes
Back to the tender thing in his charge
With clamoring tongue and taste of ashes
And a small passion to feign large.

But let his cold lips be her omen,
She shall not kiss that harried one
To peace, as men are served by women
Who comfort them in darkness and in sun.

This is the picture of a young man who has everything working for him, yet who refuses to be or cannot be the man his people and his woman need. This, Ransom tells us, is more horrible than the deaths of heroes who die nobly and less fit for the ears of ladies. The man is surrounded by beauty and joy but cares for none of it and cannot find his way anywhere because there is nowhere he cares to go.

We have noted before the ironic comparison of the "creature" to the bronze man of the ancient world who is "beaten by furies visible." The furies of the man without sense of direction are not only invisible; they are not even named. When "he is punished not knowing his sins/ And for his innocence walks in hell," we think of Dante and of the special place reserved for those who in times of crisis stay disengaged.

The man is lost though he has come from the egg of the "chosen people," the South, which people sorely need the man "Of noblest mind and powerful leg." He is lost, and we are lost a little with him, though maybe only he and his woman will know how great a loss it is.

It is a harder, a tougher poem than Ransom usually gives us. The closing lines belong to the best of the poetry he has written.

Among the most memorable of Ransom's lines are those that close his best poem of the South, "Antique Harvesters":

True, it is said of our Lady, she ageth.
But see you peep shrewdly, she hath not stooped;
Take no thought of her servitors that have dropped,
For we are nothing; and if one talk of death—
Why, the ribs of the earth subsist frail as a breath
If but God wearieth.

The Southern Calvinist preacher was never more firmly ensconced in his pulpit than in these lines.

117

A Postscript

What stays, when we have been a while with Ransom's poems, what is most clear in the consciousness, at least, is not the techniques of equilibrium, or the polarities stated; not the meanings of red or white, or the oak and its leaves. These are important and ought not to be forgotten, but what comes first to the mind, when Ransom is called up, is the language. Phrases come to mind, and they bring others to mind until our heads are filled with them. The sound of the voice is as distinctly Ransom as the signature or the picture:

> . . . Honor, Honor, they came crying . . .
> . . . A cry of Absence, Absence in the heart . . .
> . . . Translated far beyond the daughters of men . . .
> . . . Who comfort them in darkness and in sun . . .
> . . . Smoothing the heads of hungry children . . .
> . . . Who touch their quick fingers . . .

These lines come to us, and we know that the poems of Ransom comprise a poetry, a cohesive body of work. The poems speak to each other and speak to the reader in a close harmony. They come together.

119

What comes next are the people. Not even Masters populated his town more thoroughly. There are the codger Captain Carpenter and his nephew, little Max Van Vrooman. There are Conrad sitting late in his garden, his niece Margaret and his cousin Miriam. There are lovers parting; there are funerals and weddings and weddings that are funerals. There are the tall girl being led astray, the vain young scholar building delusions of grandeur, and the husband, weary and full of need, dragging himself home after a day of business.

It is in the South, somewhere east of the Mississippi and south of the Ohio, where the old mansion at the edge of town is crumbling and young men fight despair, gain patience and learn hope.

And just under the earth's crust where the town sits, we think, is Dante's hell.

Ransom builds some of his most notable images out of Dante, shaping them finely to his own ends. Dante, the Bible and classical myths are his three important sources. He reaches into each one and takes out what he needs to put a poem together, and this results sometimes in a cascade of images and metaphors that seem not to belong to the same poem; they come from such different worlds. In the best of cases, this enlivens the poem and calls from the reader a flexibility of mind the pat sequence of figures never demands.

Randall Jarrell, who was fond of listing and ranking a man's best works, put Ransom's best as "Captain Carpenter," "Antique Harvesters," "Painted Head," "Here Lies a Lady," "Judith of Bethulia," "Janet Waking," "Prelude to an Evening," Bells for John Whiteside's Daughter," "Dead Boy," "Tom, Tom, the Piper's Son," "Vision by Sweetwater," and "Old Mansion." [30]

Except for "The Vanity of the Bright Boys"—which is far from the poem Jarrell was talking about—I can accept the list of "the best" intact, as far as it goes. But I would have to add "The Equilibrists" at whichever end is supposed to be the top; and somewhere in the list would have to go "Necrological." Jarrell called "The Equilibrists," "Necrological" and "Armageddon," "mannered but fairly successful poems of an odd kind." The last, yes; the description is perfect, but the judgment on

120

"The Equilibrists" and "Necrological" are two of the only three serious miscalculations I know Jarrell to have made; the third is the failure to mention "Winter Remembered," which somehow escaped him altogether.

Of the poets of this age, only a few have been able to write love poems. Ransom is one of those few, and this poem certainly is one of the best. It will be read, along with perhaps eight or ten or a dozen other poems of Ransom's, as long as poetry is read in English. His poems will never, I think, be taken into another language successfully. For Ransom has turned the tables on Philomela; his poems are as untranslatable as her song, as American, as Calvinistic and Southern as her song is unalterably classical, and we see that Thrace is as far distant from Athens—to borrow a phrase from Diogenes—as Athens is from Thrace.

Notes

THE MAN, THE POET

1. See Ransom's *The New Criticism*, New Directions (New York, 1941); *The World's Body*, Charles Scribner's Sons (New York, 1938); and *God without Thunder*, Archon Books (Hamden, Conn., 1965). I am pleased to note here that there is no Ransom bibliography appended to this study, since the detailed and comprehensive bibliography compiled by Mildred Brooks Peters for the Louisiana State University Press publication, *John Crowe Ransom: Critical Essays and a Bibliography*, makes another effort at the compiling of a bibliography unnecessary. It is a most excellent piece of work, and students of Ransom's poetry are fortunate in having it available.

2. For many of the facts and for the proper chronology of the events mentioned on this and the following two pages, I am indebted primarily to Louise Cowan in her excellent study, *The Fugitive Group*, Louisiana State University (Baton Rouge, 1959).

3. Allen Tate, "The Fugitive—1922–1925," *Princeton University Chronicle*, III (April 1942), 83–84.

4. Foreword to *The Fugitive*, I, No. 1 (April 1922).

5. *Poetry and the Age*, Vintage Books (New York, 1955).

6. John L. Stewart, *John Crowe Ransom*, University of Minnesota Press (Minneapolis, 1962), p. 29.

7. John M. Bradbury, *The Fugitives*, Chapel Hill, 1958, p. 28.

8. *Ibid.*, p. 96.

9. "John Crowe Ransom or Thunder without God," *On Modern Poets*, Meridian Books (New York, 1959), pp. 86–87.

10. Yvor Winters or How to Measure the Wings of a Bumblebee," *Nine Essays in Modern Literature*, ed. by Don Stanford, Louisiana State University (Baton Rouge, 1965), p. 168.

11. "Problems of the Modern Critic of Literature," *The Function of Criticism*, Denver, 1957, p. 61.

12. "The Form Is the Experience," *Art Education*, XVI (October 1961), 16–22.

13. Introduction to *Southern Writing in the Sixties: Fiction*, Louisiana State University (Baton Rouge, 1966).

14. "Modern with the Southern Accent," *The Virginia Quarterly Review*, XI (April 1935), 186.

15. Louise Cowan, *The Fugitive Group*, Louisiana State University (Baton Rouge, 1959), pp. 245–246.

16. *Ibid.*, p. 246.

17. *Ibid.*, p. 235.

18. *Ibid.*

THE POET AS EQUILIBRIST

19. *Poetry and the Age*, Vintage Books (New York, 1955).

WHAT GREY MAN IS THIS?—IRONY

20. G. R. Wasserman, "The Irony of John Crowe Ransome," *The University of Kansas City Review*, XXIII, No. 2 (Dec. 1956), 151–160.

21. George Williamson, Donne and the Poetry of Today," *A Garland for John Donne*, ed. by Theodore Spencer (Cambridge, Mass., 1931).

22. Louis D. Rubin, Jr., "John Ransom's Cruel Battle," *Shenandoah*, IX (Winter 1958), pp. 23–25.

23. John M. Bradbury, "Ransom as Poet," *Accent*, XI (Winter 1951), 45–47.

24. Robert Penn Warren, "John Crowe Ransom: A Study in Irony," *The Virginia Quarterly Review*, XI, No. 1 (Jan., 1935), 93–112.

25. *The Fugitive Group: A Literary History*, Louisiana State University (Baton Rouge, 1959), p. 235.

26. Karl F. Knight, *The Poetry of John Crowe Ransom: A Study of Diction, Metaphor and Symbol,* Mouton and Company (London, 1964), p. 92.

27. *Ibid.,* p. 103.

The Thing behind the Thing: Metaphor and Other Sideway Glances

28. *Ibid.,* p. 42.

Some Other Poems

29. Philomela, the sister of Procne, was raped by Procne's husband, who was the king. So that she could not tell what had happened, he tore out her tongue. Not so easily put aside, Philomela sat at a loom and slowly wove a picture of the rape into a tapestry. When she learned the truth, the queen killed the prince Itylus, cooked him and served him to the king for vengeance. When the king, learning that he had eaten his own son, took after the sisters, the gods transformed the women into birds: Procne became a sparrow and Philomela a nightingale. The king was transformed into a hoopoe.

A Postscript

30. *Poetry and the Age,* Vintage Books, N.Y.

Miller Williams has taught at Louisiana State University, the University of Chile, Loyola University, and, as Fulbright Professor, at the National University of Mexico, and is currently Associate Professor at the University of Arkansas. He received the Henry Bellamon Poetry Award in 1957, the Bread Loaf Fellowship in Poetry in 1961, and the Amy Lowell Travelling Scholarship in Poetry for 1963–64. Founder of *The New Orleans Review* in 1968, he was also its editor until 1970. He has published four books of poems, various translations of Chilean writers, critical works, and anthologies, and has contributed to numerous periodicals and to other anthologies and texts.

The photograph facing the title page was taken by *Life Magazine* photographer Truman Moore at a party celebrating John Crowe Ransom's eightieth birthday.

The text of this book was set in Baskerville Linotype and printed by offset on P & S Special XL manufactured by P. H. Glatfelter Co., Spring Grove, Pa. Composed, printed and bound by Quinn & Boden Company, Inc., Rahway, N.J.

DATE DUE

PRINTED IN U.S.A.